Hold'em Excellence

From Beginner to Winner

Lou Krieger

ConJelCo
Pittsburgh, Pennsylvania

Hold'em Excellence: From Beginner to Winner
Copyright © 2000 by Lou Krieger

Publisher's Cataloging-in-Publication Data

Krieger, Lou

Hold'em Excellence: From Beginner to Winner
xii, 199 p. : ill. ; 22 cm.
ISBN 1-886070-14-8
I. Title.

Library of Congress Catalog Card Number: 00-106647

Second Edition

5 7 9 8 6

Cover design by Lisa M. Lane

ConJelCo LLC
132 Radcliff Drive
Pittsburgh, PA 15237
[412] 492-9210
http://www.conjelco.com

This book is dedicated to the memory of Moke and Tobby, whose bright, shining season in the sun was all too brief.

Table of Contents

Acknowledgements

I feel fortunate indeed for all the help and assistance I received in preparing, editing, and publishing this book. I wish to thank Mike Caro, Natalie Jones, and Rick Nebiolo for reviewing the contents. All of these individuals — in addition to being talented poker players — think extensively about the game and were willing to share and discuss their viewpoints, beliefs, and opinions with me.

Thanks to June Field for taking a chance on a new voice and bringing me on board as a columnist for *Card Player* magazine. Thanks also to the present staff at the magazine, especially to Linda Johnson, Jan Fisher, Bonnie Rattner, and Steve Radulovich for their encouragement, and to Nolan Dalla, who is always available with a word of wisdom, a fine idea, and an incredible way with words.

I am indebted to my original partners in this project, June Field and Maryann Guberman. The latter has met more production deadlines than even she would care to recall as production manager for the *Card Player* and numerous other publications. Thanks also to Lynne Loomis, a talented editor and poker player who, through the early days of the book's manuscript gracefully sprinkled seeds of articulation over my own awkwardly chosen words and caused them to bloom. Finally, thanks to my current publisher, Chuck Weinstock. Without the combined talents of these individuals, my efforts alone would not have flourished.

The truth is rarely pure, and never simple.
—Oscar Wilde

You Can Learn to Play a Top-Notch Game of Texas Hold'em

Do you want to play Texas hold'em poker and excel at it? If you've been a lifetime low-limit player, I can show you the skills you'll need to move up to bigger games — and win. Even if you've never played the game before, I can teach you how to play, and play well.

Poker Skills Can be Taught — and Learned

Before I fill your heart with enthusiasm, and your head with visions of megabucks merrily dancing across a card table onto your stack of chips, consider this: *It won't be easy.* I can provide the knowledge and strategies you'll need to be a winner. But you'll have to contribute the effort, discipline, and mental toughness no winner can do without.

Poker is extremely competitive and requires a great deal of skill to play well. While you'll find the information in this book potent stuff, it's not enough. Not by a longshot. To really succeed you'll need to read, to study, and especially to think critically and analytically about poker when you're away from the table.

Of course, you'll need game experience too. As batting practice is *not* baseball, reading about poker, or playing against computerized opponents — while undeniably helpful — is *not* the same as playing for real money, against live opponents, in public games. By studying the fundamentals provided in this book, however, you'll avoid mistakes most players with years of experience habitually make.

If you've been playing for years but never *studied* the game before, congratulations. You're taking the first step toward significantly upgrading your knowledge and skills. If you're a newcomer, rest easy. You've no bad habits to overcome.

Learning to play well means paying your dues in live games. There's no reason to make it expensive, however, since most casinos and cardrooms offer a variety of games at lower limits. If you're new to poker, start there. You'll know when you're ready to test your mettle in bigger games. Like any new player, you're likely to feel intimidated venturing into a public game, so I'll give you enough information to make your transition comfortable, and I'll provide the know-how for winning.

I learned to play exactly as I'm suggesting you learn. I bought books. I studied and even memorized parts of them. And I played, played, played. I didn't read the poker books just once. I've literally worn out some of them. You'll need to do the same. Eventually you'll move up through this iterative spiral of know-how and experience to find you're a pretty darned good player.

For the past decade I've written a column called "On Strategy" in *Card Player* — the most widely circulated poker publication in the world. I've received letters and e-mail from readers in Pocatello, Idaho and Paris, France. While there's no shortage of poker books, the players reading my column, as well as those responding to *Card Player* reader surveys convinced me of the need for a comprehensive, easy-to-understand book about hold'em — one designed to take a player from the basics all the way up through the skills required to play and win in public cardrooms.

Texas hold'em is the fastest growing game in poker. With the continued growth of legalized card casinos around the world, and virtual casinos in cyberspace where one can play real poker for real money, the expansion of Texas hold'em has been phenomenal. Most of us who grew up on kitchen-table stud poker have now become strong advocates of this faster-paced game. It's more fun, and doesn't require memorizing discards.

In public cardrooms you can play against some of the toughest players anywhere. But they're not all tough. Once you learn to recognize them, some players are begging you to take their money. Spotting a weak game and capitalizing on it can be learned. I'll show you how.

Winning money is a terrific feeling. In fact, there's a wonderful bit of dialogue in the film *The Color of Money* when Paul Newman's character utters this immortal line: "Money won is twice as sweet as money earned!

What You'll Learn From This Book

- How hold'em is played in public cardrooms.

- Why game selection is critical.

- Why choosing a bad game can make even a skilled player an underdog.

- Grouping starting hands according to quality.

- How to assess hands from a variety of perspectives.

- Why hands often change dramatically in value on the flop.

- What to do with each kind of flop you encounter.

- How to extract the maximum profit when you have a big hand.

- How to deduce what you opponents might be holding.

- Dealing with common plays encountered on the turn.

- What to do when picking up a draw on the turn that complements your hand.

- When to try for a check-raise and when to bet.

- When is an outright bluff worth a try?

- What is a semibluff, and when to go for one?

- Whether to come out betting or try for a check-raise when you make your draw.

- Popular theories of money management (such as setting stop-loss limits, and quitting once you've won some predetermined amount) will be debunked.

- Analyses you can and should be doing at the table.

- Determining your opponent's probable hand by analyzing his betting patterns.

- Playing in spread-limit games.

- How spread-limit games offer golden opportunities to play "bargain" hands.

- Practical benefits of working with computerized hold'em software programs.

- Keeping records: what information to collect, and how to gather it.

- Simple statistical methods for analyzing data and using that information to improve your game.

- How to make a firm and binding commitment to winning.

- Additional knowledge and strategic concepts you should acquire in your continuous quest for growth and development as a poker player.

- How your newly acquired poker skills have value in other aspects of your life.

Does this sound exciting? Do you want to learn how to play a top-notch game of Texas hold'em? You can — if you're not afraid of a lot of hard work and effort. C'mon along. They're starting to deal the cards.

— Lou Krieger

by Mike Caro, "America's Mad Genius"

*L*ou Krieger knows the truth. I'm not talking about some puny little particle of truth. I'm talking about the fundamental truth that governs the poker universe. I teach it, Lou Krieger teaches it on these pages, and anyone who doesn't understand it, doesn't win.

So, listen carefully, because here comes the truth: "In poker, good players beat bad players." And that simple truth makes poker different from other forms of gambling that nobody can beat, such as craps and roulette. In poker, it matters what decisions you make, and your long-term performance will be a direct reflection of the quality of your decisions.

Good players don't just beat bad players, but the best ones win consistently all their lives, all across America. Because poker combines skill and luck, bad players will sometimes win, and good players will sometimes lose. There's no getting around that, but that's a good thing. If weak opponents never won, they'd never play. It's hoping that they might get lucky and win today that makes weak players pour profit into your pockets.

Once you realize that good players really do beat bad players, you have to discover how to be a good player. This book tells you. Lou Krieger defines and clarifies the core strategies that can turn a beginner into a winner. In my seminars, I explain that winning is just a matter of making quality decisions at the poker table. If you consistently make better decisions than your opponents, you'll eventually win. This book tells you how to make those winning decisions, and it's packed with precise examples that can earn money for you immediately.

When Lou asked me to write this preface, I didn't even hesitate. He's a man who practices what he preaches, and his results at the poker table clearly prove his point. We both play regularly in the cardrooms of Southern California, mostly at Hollywood Park Casino. Whenever I walk by a game that Lou Krieger is in, it's a good bet he has more chips than he started with. Winning, after all, is what it's all about. And Lou Krieger is a consistent winner at hold'em.

If you've never played poker seriously before, reading this book — or any other poker book — might not turn you into a big winner overnight. You'll need to get a feel for how to apply these tactics by playing in live games. But this book is an amazing shortcut for beginners. And it will even enhance the play of experienced players.

You'll find something of value on almost every page. I believe the illustrations of which hold'em starting hands should be played, by position, is worth more than the price of the book all by itself. Take it from "the Mad Genius," reading this book is an investment in your future at the poker table. And that, too, is the truth.

Mike Caro, more commonly known as "the Mad Genius of Poker" or "America's Mad Genius," is often regarded as today's foremost authority on poker strategy, psychology, and statistics.

"Money won is twice as sweet as money earned."

Paul Newman as Fast Eddie in *The Color of Money*

Part One:

Basic Education

If they're helpless and they can't defend themselves,
you're in the right game.

Mike Caro

Chapter 1

Just a few years ago poker was legal only in Washington, Montana, Oregon, Nevada, and California. But not anymore. Look around. From Maryland to Mississippi and Michigan to New Mexico, poker is played everywhere. If you want to play you can find a game on a replica of a 19th century paddle wheel riverboat or on Native American tribal lands. Poker is played in two-table, no-frills cardrooms and elegant Los Angeles County megaclubs, where 150 games with betting limits ranging from $1-$2 to $200-$400 are going simultaneously.

In the past few years poker has exploded. Stud and hold'em were legally played in only a few locales until quite recently. Now these games are as common as corn.

This book is aimed at readers who are new to casino poker, though not necessarily new to the game itself. If you've played in home games, but have yet to make the transition to casino poker, this chapter is especially for you. If you are new to poker, or very inexperienced, you should also read *Poker for Dummies*, which I wrote with Richard D. Harroch.

Playing in a Casino

Casino poker is different from home poker, and while a home game may be long on both camaraderie and unusual variants of the game, there are many reasons to play in a public cardroom. The most important is simply this: *There is always a game.* Often, there's a choice of games. If you're in one of the giant cardrooms, not only will there always be a game, but there usually will be a choice of games at every betting level. These games will be available twenty-four hours a day, seven days a week. Your home game, by comparison, probably goes one night a week — at best.

Another major advantage, especially in urban locations, is the safety of public cardrooms. They offer professional dealers, floorpersons, and video security the equal of any Las Vegas casino to ensure that games are run squarely. Because people walk around cardrooms with large sums of money, there are more security guards than you'd find in a dozen banks. Parking lots are brightly lit, well-patrolled and free of strong-arm crime. Since most large clubs offer player banks, check cashing and ATM machines, you do not have to walk in or out of these clubs with large sums of money in your pocket.

In a public cardroom there is no pressure to stay. Nobody minds if you quit the game a winner. Someone else is usually waiting for your seat. You do, however, have to pay to play. Whether the game is paid for by time collection or by raking the pot, it will cost you more to play in a casino than in a home game — where all you have to do is split the cost of food and drinks. In Los Angeles, where I play, it costs $6 per half-hour to sit in a $15-$30 hold'em game. When I calculate my hourly average winnings, I have to overcome the $12 per hour I pay to sit in the game, plus tips to the dealer (called a "toke" in casino parlance) whenever I win sufficiently sized pots, before I am "in profit." If I'm able to beat a $15-$30 hold'em game at a rate of $25 per hour, it is the equivalent of beating a home game for $35 per hour before paying for my share of the refreshments.

In a cardroom I can play when I want to, in my choice of games and at the limits I prefer. If there are weak players in my game, I can punish them continuously. Weak players in home games eventually become ex-players if they can't win some of the time. Cardrooms offer a variety. If I don't like the hold'em games, I can play stud, lowball, or Omaha high-low split. Those kinds of choices are seldom available in home games.

As a cardroom newcomer, you'll find the games are played differently than they are at home. Initially, they will seem much faster. Absent is that slow and easy banter that exists in a home game. While there is chatter at the table, the dealer will try to maintain a quick pace. If you are playing in a game with a time collection, you are paying the same fee per half-hour, regardless of how many hands are played. Consequently, dealers act efficiently and players are expected to make prompt decisions.

Things you've probably done in home games just won't happen in a cardroom. No one ever fishes through the discards. The dealer handles the deck. You play your cards.

Table Stakes — Cards Speak
Rules are interpreted strictly and consistently. Games are table stakes and cards speak. Table stakes means you can only play with

the money you had on the table when that hand was dealt. You are not permitted to go light as you might in a home game. If you do not have enough to cover the bets and raises, you go *all in*. You are then simply contesting the portion of the pot that your money covers. Wagers can still be made by other players active in that hand, but those bets comprise a side pot. At the end of the hand, the side pot is decided first, then the main pot. You are not eligible to win the side pot since you invested no money in it, however, you can win the main pot. At any time between hands you can buy more chips or put more money on the table.

Few things you remember from Saturday matinee Westerns happen in a public cardroom. Players do not leave the game in mid-hand, go get the deed to the ranch, then use it to cover a bet. You cannot drive someone out of a pot just by betting more money than he has in front of him. The player with the limited chip supply can go all in — by calling with the remainder of his chips. If the all-in player loses, he either buys more chips or leaves the game.

You'll also notice that no one ever says: "...Mighty big bet, cowboy. I'll just see your twenty," while reaching back into his stack for more chips, and with a long, lingering glance for effect, drawls "...and raise you forty!" Calling a bet, then reaching back for more chips without announcing a raise is called a string raise. It is not permitted. Rest assured someone will shout "String raise!" The dealer will then inform the hopeful raiser that a string raise just occurred, and he'll have to take his raise back and simply call. Now, if someone shouts "String raise!" and your opponent says something like "That's OK. Let the raise stand," be assured your hand is in big trouble. Real big trouble!

This rule prevents a player from reading the reactions of his opponents while he puts some chips in the pot, then deciding to raise if he thinks he's got the best of it. If you want to raise, just say "Raise." Then you can go back to your stack and count out the proper amount of chips. If you want to let your action announce your intention, you must put the correct amount of chips into the pot all in one motion. Otherwise it's a string raise.

You don't want to "splash" the pot either by tossing chips into the center of the table where they mingle with the others. Instead, stack your chips neatly on the table about eighteen inches in front of you. The dealer will pull them into the pot when the action has been completed on that round of betting.

If it's your first time in a public cardroom, tell the dealer so he can help you through the mechanics of the game. After a few sessions, you will be familiar and comfortable with the majority of playing procedures. You'll soon feel like a regular.

In a casino, unlike in many home games, you are always responsible for the protection of your hand. Toss it in the discards, or *muck*, and your hand is fouled. It cannot win. If you are unsure of whether you hold the winning hand at the showdown, turn it face up and let the dealer read your hand. The rule in all cardrooms is *cards speak*. Dealers, however, can make mistakes. If you think you hold the best hand, turn it over and announce it. Place it halfway between your chips and the pot, and hold on to it while the dealer determines the outcome.

Anytime you are uncertain of an action, the best procedure is to call "Time!" This freezes the action. Then have your questions answered prior to acting. Poker etiquette suggests that you not abuse this privilege, particularly if you are in a game where you are charged by the half-hour. It's not as cardinal a sin in a game that is raked, but players usually want a fast, efficiently-run game, with as few interruptions as possible.

Decks are changed frequently in cardrooms. In home games the same deck might be used all night — and again next week. In Los Angeles, for example, they change decks every half-hour. In addition, players unhappy with their run of cards are prone to holler "Deck change!" Most cardrooms permit a change once a deck has been in play for an entire round.

You may never have noticed, but the shuffle procedure is probably less than adequate in your home game. Home game players are usually unfamiliar with the mechanics of a good shuffle and lack the manual dexterity to perform one due to their lack of experience.

Well-trained casino dealers assemble the deck so the cards face the players, frequently preceding that by scrambling the cards on the table. They will then go through a four-step process of shuffle, shuffle, riffle, shuffle. Finally, the dealer cuts the deck and deals. It's efficient, quick, and no cards are flashed in the process.

In a cardroom, you won't find some of the games you play at home. In fact, there are no wild-card games in public cardrooms. Only draw and lowball are played with a 53-card deck. That additional card is a *joker*. It is usable in draw only as an ace or to complete a straight or flush. In lowball, the joker is used as the lowest card not already in your hand. You won't find deuces or one-eyed jacks wild. Nor will you find the bizarre assortment of games home players create when they're losing, and want to stimulate enough action to help them get even in the last, long hours before dawn.

How to Get in a Game

Now that you understand some of the differences between home and casino poker, how do you get in a game? When you enter a cardroom, you may see a white board full of players' initials. These initials are listed under games that are available. For example, if you walk into a large Los Angeles cardroom, you might find seven players ahead of you waiting for the $2-$4 hold'em game. Just give your initials to the board attendant and indicate the games you would like to play. You might say: "My initials are ABC. Put me up for the $2-$4 and $3-$6 hold'em, the $5-$10 stud, and the $4-$8 Omaha high-low split games."

That's all there is to it. Your initials will go up on the board for each game you requested. You'll be called as seats become available. If the board for a particular game is so long that the club can start another one, the attendant will announce that game, and call the first eight or nine players listed. When you hear your initials, go to the table and take the vacant seat. *You're in the game.*

Some cardrooms do not use a board. Just give your initials or first name to the floorperson or *brush* and tell him the games you want to play. In small cardrooms, where there are only one or two tables, ask the dealer if a seat is available or if there is a wait list for the game.

When you first sit in the game either the floorperson or dealer will ask you how much you want in chips. Each game has a minimum buy-in. Give him your money and you'll get your chips. Large casinos have chip attendants. One of them will take your money, announce to the table that "Seat five (or whatever seat you occupy) is playing $200 behind." That means you bought in for $200 and the casino is in the process of fetching your chips. You can play that hand, even though your chips have not yet arrived. The dealer will either lend you chips or keep count of how much you owe the pot. Your chips should arrive before that first hand is played to its conclusion.

What Will Your Opponents Be Like?

Now that you're playing in a public cardroom, what kinds of players are likely to be sitting at your table? It depends on the limits you play. If you play in low-limit games, you are not going to find last year's *World Series of Poker* winner, the eight toughest card players in your hometown, or any legends of the game. While there are many ways to classify players as you try to build a book on your opponents, the easiest way to do this initially is to group your opponents into three types: Casual recreational players, regulars, or professionals.

Casual Recreational Players

Casual recreational players love the game, but when push comes to shove, they are not that concerned about winning or losing. They play for fun. It is simply a hobby and no matter how much they lose, it is less expensive than keeping horses, restoring classic automobiles, or a hundred other hobbies that devour money. Naturally, you'd love to play exclusively with recreational players. If you can't beat a table full of these players, you might just want to find something else to do in your spare time. No one, however, will come right out and admit to being a casual recreational player. If he does, watch out. He probably is not. Be forewarned: Take heed when he fires a raise at you.

Cardroom Regulars

Most players are regulars. They come in a wide variety. Some are similar in skill level to casual recreational players but are at the cardroom every day. They may think they beat the game, but they probably do not win much — if at all. Others may be retired and playing on their pension. Among the regulars you'll also find housewives, students, people with no fixed job hours, and dealers who are playing before or after their shift. Some regulars have independent sources of income and often play in big games. Take it for a fact that all the regulars you encounter will have more playing experience than you. Even if you are a stronger player, but are just making the transition from home games to casino poker, they will have the best of it for a while. After all, they are in playing shape. You, on the other hand, are in spring training and need some time to adjust to this entirely new environment.

Regulars comprise the vast majority of players. Some are good. Most aren't. But they're in action on a regular basis. As you begin to refine your player categories, it is this category of regulars you'll be subdividing.

Professionals

Professionals and semiprofessionals will be found in most of the larger games. Generally speaking, you will not encounter them at limits below $10-$20. While a pro would have an easier time of it at lower betting limits, he just can't earn a living in a $2-$4 game. In these lower-limit games, you'll be competing with regulars and recreational players, not professionals. But when you graduate to the higher limits, you can expect to encounter some players who earn their living playing poker.

You need not be afraid of a pro or two in your game. Because they usually play good, steady poker, they can be a stabilizing influence in games that otherwise might be very loose. While a good player will ultimately earn more money in a very loose game, the fact that each pot has a multitude of active players in it, and is often raised and reraised, means that the element of short term luck is stronger.

The result: Players in loose games suffer larger fluctuations along their road to success. A pro or two will stabilize these loose games, if for no other reason than they won't be betting and raising every hand. Consequently, while their win rate might not be as great in balanced games, they do not need as large a bankroll to sustain themselves. And neither will you.

Proposition Players

Another category of player is the proposition player, or "prop." Props play on their own money but are paid a salary by the house to help start or "prop up" games. You'll typically find them late at night when the club is trying to keep games going, and early in the morning when it's trying to start up a new game.

The life of a prop can be tough. He plays in short-handed games, or games struggling to get off the ground. The minute a live player wants his seat, the prop is pulled from it — often when the game is just starting to bear fruit. Props typically play better than most regulars, but not as good as top players. Their defining character-istic is that they tend to play conservatively.

Many cardroom newcomers panic at the thought of a prop in their game. Since the props are paid by the casino, players often believe they have a big advantage. Not true. They play their own money, and as long as they're reliable and do not insult the clientele, management is happy with them. So long as they maintain a playing bankroll the house cares not a whit whether they win or lose. I suspect that given a choice, any cardroom would prefer to employ a weak player as a prop, rather than a strong one, simply because the weaker player is a bigger draw. In fact, the ideal prop would be a losing player, with a winning personality and an unlimited bankroll.

Public Poker Is Different Than Home Games

If you've watched a few games while waiting for a seat, you'll notice that players do not play as many hands as they do in home games. While there is seldom a spoken agreement to play every hand in a home game, because of the chummy atmosphere, many times there is an implied agreement to play most hands.

That's not the case in a casino. Players are more selective. Still, the biggest mistakes most players make are playing too many hands and calling on early betting rounds when they should have folded.

Coming from a home game into a casino, this may seem like a paradox. It's not. Even if you think your regular home game is tough, take it on faith — at least for now — that your home game is much too loose. Moreover, low-limit cardroom games, while tighter than your home game, are also much too loose. If you simply play better starting cards than your opponents do in these low-limit games, you will be a favorite.

However, you'll not be a favorite in any game right off the mark. Since it will take you some time to get familiar with cardroom play, give serious consideration to starting in very small-limit games. You'll probably be paying for lessons the first five to ten times you play in a public cardroom, and there is no reason to make these lessons any more expensive than they need be.

In moving from a home game into a public cardroom, especially the fun-to-play, jam-it-up kind of home game, you'll quickly realize that you cannot play every hand, or even many hands, for that matter! You need standards. This is true for all forms of poker.

Bobby Baldwin, former world champion of poker, reflecting about his early days at the table said, "I was floating around, trying to figure out which hands were playable, which hands called for a raise, which hands should be thrown out." Without standards, he said, "… you have to use 90 percent of your concentration deciding each time what to do with a given hand. All that mental energy should be devoted to studying your opponents and trying to decipher the small things which made this hand slightly different from familiar hands you've seen in the past."

Baldwin's advice is succinct. "Never sit in a game without having a preconceived set of guidelines telling you what your minimum calling hands and raising hands should be."

The speed of the games when you first play in a cardroom might startle you. You may think that all of the players are better than your home game cronies. Still, after becoming familiar with a cardroom environment, you'll find your skill level is right up there with your opponents. However, the majority of your opponents are not students of the game. Recreational players don't really care. They want to have fun and that's it. Most of the regulars, who run the gamut of skill levels, do not bother to study the game. Though many of them have been playing in cardrooms for years, they simply repeat and reinforce the same errors they've been making for decades.

Don't worry too much about the skill level of your opponents when you first begin playing in a public cardroom. By studying and playing the game you should soon catch the field. Mind you, if you live in an area in which poker has only recently been legalized, you probably do not have any catching up to do at all. You can start ahead of the crowd and never look back. Think of yourself as a wire-to-wire winner. Your opponents may improve slowly, simply through osmosis. But through frequent play and study, you'll be improving at a much more rapid rate.

Chapter 2

The Game of Texas Hold'em

Why Play Hold'em?

Texas hold'em is the most popular game played in many public cardrooms. While stud may still be more popular in Atlantic City and at Foxwoods, in Connecticut, hold'em is gaining ground.

According to poker author Ray Zee, "Texas hold'em is hard! There is probably no other form of poker as difficult. Yet the game appears to be deceptively simple." Part of hold'em's appeal is its apparent simplicity. Because of the communal cards in the middle of the table, you need not remember what other players might have tossed away when they folded their hands. The game is typically played with a minimum of nine players at a table, and appears to be a faster, more action-filled game than stud.

So why play hold'em? According to Zee, "Many players, even after much experience at the poker tables, still play like any two cards can win. Of course," he adds, "those who play in this fashion quickly lose their money." Hold'em is the game used to determine the champion at the World Series of Poker, and it is the fastest growing poker game in the world.

If You've Never Played Hold'em Before

While on the surface hold'em may look like seven-card stud, it is quite different. For those readers who have never played hold'em, here is a very quick review of the game procedures. The house dealer deals around the table until each player has two cards. There is a round of betting. Then three communal cards, called the flop, are turned face up in the center of the table. There is another round of betting. Then a fourth communal card (called the turn) is exposed. A round of betting again takes place. Then the fifth, and final piece of community property (referred to as the river card) is placed in the center of the table followed by final round of betting. The best hand made using any combination of a player's two hole cards and the five communal cards is the winner.

A button rotates around the table after each hand, signifying the "dealer" for that hand. The player with the dealer button acts last.

Unlike stud, where position is determined by the cards showing on the board, the player with the dealer button acts last in every round of betting — with the exception of the first one. The two players immediately to the left of the button must post blind bets on the first round only to begin the action. In a $10-$20 hold'em game, for example, the blinds are $5 and $10. Each is a live blind. Because these blinds are a forced, first bet, they can raise when the betting has gone around the table and it is their turn to act again (but only on the first round).

Since the order in which players act is fixed throughout the game, hold'em is considered a "positional" game. Acting last, after you've had an opportunity to see how your opponents play, is a significant advantage.

Poker author Mason Malmuth says, "Most of your luck occurs early in hold'em, while most of your luck occurs late in stud." In hold'em you have seen five of your seven cards by the flop — which is the second round of betting. By the second round of betting in stud you've only looked at four of your cards, and you have three more rounds of betting to go. "The amount of luck in hold'em is minimized" according to Malmuth, because "... when the board pairs, both you and your opponent add that pair to your hands (assuming that this card does not make either of you a set, or perhaps a flush)."

Because luck is minimized, top hold'em players can win more money while putting less of their bankroll at risk. To succeed at hold'em, the first decision you'll make is crucial. "What cards," you must ask yourself, "am I going to stay with"?

You'll hear players tell you "Any two cards can win." That's usually uttered when some player in the big blind holding a K-2 calls a raised pot and sees the flop come 2-2-K and proceeds to shred the raiser who's holding an A-K. At hold'em, especially at the lower limits, you'll find some players who habitually take the flop with almost any two cards from any position. They may be playing tighter than you've been used to at home, but they are still *gambling*, and playing far too many hands.

The classic distinction between gambling and poker was made by Anthony Holden in his book: *Big Deal: A Year As a Professional Poker Player*. "Poker ..." mused Holden, better known in literary circles as the biographer of Laurence Olivier and the Prince of

Wales, "was not a form of gambling; on the contrary, gambling was a style of playing poker — a loose and losing style, at that."

You expect the best hands after the flop in hold'em to hold up, so it is frustrating when you're holding premium cards but keep losing to weak players who run you down. But you're not alone, and you'll hear more than your share of bad-beat stories at the hold'em table.

Success at hold'em demands that you be patient, pay close attention to position, and understand that in spite of the bad-beat stories, the best hold'em hands are run down less often than the best seven-card stud hands.

Continuous Improvement is the Key

If you want to sound worldly, tell your friends your hold'em style is based on *Kai-zen*, a Japanese management philosophy. A key element of *Kai-zen* is that your business must improve at a more rapid rate than that of your competition — catching, and passing them, yet striving all the while for continuous improvement. If you are a serious poker player, or even an aspiring poker player who wants to become a serious one, *Kai-zen* — or continuous improvement — is a principle to build into your game plan.

Everyone starts somewhere. Usually that somewhere is nowhere near the finish line. If you're going to become a good poker player and savor all the opportunities and enjoyment that can be had in a public cardroom, you should set your sights on continuous improvement. You'll find your abilities and confidence as a poker player will grow.

Remember this: The toughest decision you will have made is that first one — the decision to play in a cardroom. Within a short period of time you'll feel comfortable with the games and with your ability. From that point forward, you'll go as far and fast as your skill, dedication, and self-discipline will carry you.

Your home game will still be there. Become a better player and you'll be able to run over it if you want to. Or play it for fun. Now that you have made the decision to play in a public cardroom — be it that Native American casino or riverboat scheduled to open in your area — go on and do it. Say the magic words, "Deal me in!"

Chapter 3

Essential Strategic Considerations

*I*n his book *Poker Essays*, Mason Malmuth says that a great $10–$20 hold'em player could expect to win an average of $35 per hour. If you're a $2–$4 player that might translate to $7 per hour. If you play $3–$6, excellent play might earn $10.50. The question is, of course, what constitutes great play — and how can it be achieved.

If you are currently a winning player at any level, you probably realize that perfect play is probably unachievable. But even near-perfect play, world-class play, or great play goes a lot further than simply never allowing yourself to go on tilt, bluffing and calling at an appropriate frequency, playing the right starting hands in various positions, and seeking out the best games.

Top notch play also means that you need to apply strategic concepts in a dynamic fashion. Consequently, the strategies you choose must be considered in relation to the current game situation. If you expect to be able to play great poker, you need to have a thorough knowledge of basic poker strategy. Once you understand basic strategic concepts, then you need to learn how and when to adjust them for changing game situations.

Basic strategic knowledge is critical for any poker player. If you have no basis for making decisions about whether to call, fold, raise, or reraise, then you might just as well play the lottery. Sure, you'll win occasionally, but you'll exercise no control over your destiny as a card player.

First Learn the Basics

Your first efforts should center around learning basic poker concepts. Once you are a proven winning player, you can concern yourself with learning to play very well. It is also important to realize that even when you know and understand the basics, this know-how must be continuously applied. The knowledge and abilities that comprise basic poker skills are not a pill to be swallowed once. Your medication must be taken on a prescribed basis for life.

Andres Segovia, the classical guitarist, reputedly spent four to six hours per day (of his six-to-eight-hour practice day) playing scales. Think about it. The greatest classical guitarist of his generation did not spend the majority of his practice time learning new pieces or practicing his concert repertoire. He did just what beginning music students do. He played scales. He spent 75 percent of his practice time on the basics, and he did this every day.

About ten years ago I read a book titled *Conceptual Blockbusting*. It dealt with the techniques of problem solving. One of the author's main points is this: The way in which a problem is defined often has a great deal to do with the solution. This is referred to as "bounding" the problem, and bounding issues come up all the time at the poker table.

Are you, for instance, attempting to win the most pots or win the most money? If you think that you are there to win the most pots, your strategy will be very, very different from what it will be if you are trying to win the most money. If your objective is to win every pot, just play every pot. You'll win every pot you could possibly win, but you'll soon be broke and watching the game from the rail.

If you want to win the most money, be selective, be aggressive when it's warranted, and you have a chance to win big.

You can see clearly from this very simple example that the way in which you defined or "bounded" the problem pointed you strongly in the direction of one — or another — strategic choice.

Don't Get Discouraged.
Even Big-Time Pros Make Mistakes

Even world-class professionals make the mistake of "bounding a problem incorrectly." This situation occurred a few years ago at the final table of the main event at the Bicycle Club Casino's *Diamond Jim Brady Tournament*.

Three players remained: At that point, Player X had almost twice the number of chips as either Players Y or Z (who were approximately equal in chip position). The payoffs were as follows: $230,000 to the winner of the tournament, $115,000 for second place, and $55,200 for third. In a heads-up situation against Player X, Player Y went all in on the flop when two diamonds fell giving him a flush draw.

It was all or nothing for Player Y the moment he made the decision to go all in and draw for the flush. If the flush came, Player Y would win the hand, double his stack, and be solidly ensconced in second place. If his flush didn't fall he would be out of the tournament. With two cards to come he had a 35 percent chance of making his hand and a 65 percent chance of busting out of the tournament.

Even if he did win that hand, however, there was no guarantee he would win the tournament or even capture second place. Thus he allowed himself to take a position as a 1.9-to-1 underdog in a situation where, even if he overcame those odds, he had no guarantee of a higher payoff in the tournament. As it happened, Player Y's flush never came, while Player Z made a remarkable comeback and went on to defeat Player X, who had been the chip leader.

The big winner in the confrontation between Players X and Y was Player Z. He went from a virtual tie for second/third place to a guarantee of second-place money. That was a difference of $59,800. Remember, Player Z, who had absolutely nothing at risk in that confrontation, would have been a winner regardless of the result. With Player Y knocked out of the tournament, Player Z guaranteed himself a payoff that was $59,800 more than he could count on before that hand was played. If Player Y won the hand, then Player Z would have still been in third place, but Player X would no longer have a big chip lead and no longer be in a position to hammer the shorter stacks.

Why would a top tournament player make the strategic decision to contest that pot as an underdog when the risk clearly outweighed the reward? It is very likely that Player Y was so focused on the situation at hand that he was, in that instant, unable to step back and grasp the issue in its broadest context. If that's the case, he simply was not aware that Player Z also had a major stake in the outcome of that hand, even though he held no cards!

Just this momentary lack of awareness, entirely understandable when you consider the intense concentration required to survive as one of three finalists in a $10,000 buy-in, no-limit hold'em tournament, could easily lead to an error in correctly bounding a problem. In so doing, the wrong strategy was selected.

While strategy late in a tournament can be very different than the tactics you'd apply in a regular game (also referred to as a "ring" game), the point of this discussion was not to make you a better tournament player. That's not the focus of this book. I want to make you aware of the need to look at poker problems from a variety of perspectives. *Step back and see the big picture.* Then examine the nitty-gritty details. Somewhere there's a perspective appropriate for your strategic objectives.

That's the reason it's occasionally correct, when you're up against good opponents, to purposely misplay a hand, or otherwise act out of character. A good player will make a mental note of your bad play, and you can use it to your advantage later on. But don't use this kind of advertising against bad players. They probably won't take heed of what you've done and you'll have cost yourself money and gotten no value from your attempted ploy.

You Have to Know Your Opponents

What about this situation: You've learned a lot about poker simply by virtue of having read all the really good poker books. Not only have you read them, but you also clearly understand the strategic concepts they contain. Now you want to continuously improve your poker skills by applying these concepts at the table.

So you sit in a game with familiar faces, and you know you'll love it. You see a couple of timid and cautious (weak-tight) players and three players who seldom fold and hate it when they do. They're real "calling stations." You're dealt

in seat No. 7. You raise and are called by the big blind and a calling station in seat No. 5. The flop comes

"Fantastic," you say to yourself, "I've got position, two overcards, and a nut-flush draw." You remember something about semibluffing and implied odds, and when the big blind and seat No. 5 check the flop, you bet. They both call.

The turn brings the

and it's checked to you. You bet, thinking about that semibluff.

Maybe they'll fold and you can win it right here. Maybe you even have the best hand and would win in a showdown right now. Perhaps a heart will come on the river not only making your flush, but the best possible or "nut flush." But you are up against two players who sleep very well, thank you, each and every night of the week, secure in the knowledge that no one, but no one, ever steals a pot from them.

The river is no help. It's the

Both players check to you again. You still might have the best hand if you show it down. But you bet and you're called, and you lose to one of the calling stations who shows you a 6–5 of mixed suits.

"What went wrong?" you ask yourself. "I had the perfect opportunity to semibluff." Perfect, that is, only from the perspective of the cards on the table and those in your hand. But it was far from perfect if you stopped to consider your opponents.

Your mistake involved considering only the cards while bounding the problem and choosing a strategy. *Semibluffing doesn't work with calling stations.* You have to show a calling station the best hand to take the money. While there is nothing you could have done to win that pot, you certainly could have saved a bet on the river.

There was nothing wrong with the strategy itself. It might have worked if the cards were the same but with different opponents. Remember, you need to know your opponents at least as well as you understand strategic concepts.

Strategy and Situational Dependency

In fact, the entire point of dynamically-applied strategies is that strategy is dependent on situations.

The key to dynamic strategies is to keep adjusting and modifying the dimensions of the problems encountered at the poker table to enable you to think of them from a variety of perspectives. Be aware of the big picture while simultaneously paying attention to small details.

Understanding strategic concepts is only part of the battle. How, and under what circumstances you apply them is equally important. If you are able to do this, you will find that you have become a better, more solid player — as well as a more creative one.

Preparing to Win

Every poker player would like to win. But wishing and hoping are not enough. Knowledge by itself won't get you there. Success demands preparation for winning. That usually means making behavioral changes while ridding yourself of poorly-learned habits and old paradigms. Knowledge, plus preparation, equals *know-how*, and that's what it takes. If you have that knowledge and you're losing, or you're just not winning as much and as often as you should, look toward changing your behavior or habits. Here are some steps you can take.

Be Responsible for Yourself

Don't ask for a deck change. New cards won't help. And the dealer is not responsible for the cards you're dealt or how you play them. You are responsible for yourself. Step one in making behavioral changes and eliminating bad habits is the irrevocable assumption that you are personally responsible for what happens to you at the poker table. If you put the blame on forces outside yourself, you have not committed yourself to making changes; you're just denying the problem. Come back when you grow up!

If the Shoe Fits, Steal It!

Find a role model, or better yet, a couple of them. Watch players whose results you admire and try to find out what they do and how they do it. See if you can learn the secrets of their discipline. Learn how they resist the temptation to play marginal hands in bad positions. Determine how they keep from going on tilt, and discover how they exploit the table when they have the best of it.

I have a friend who is a very successful mid-limit hold'em player. When he takes a bad beat — one that gets to him emotionally — he gets up from the table and walks around the casino. I've even seen him pace the parking lot. This enables him to cool down and regain his composure. Some people think it's foolish, but he is a consistent winner and he's in the game every day. His critics are frequently on the rail.

If you feel yourself losing self-control, you'll need to develop some method for regaining control. Going on tilt, and steaming your bankroll away can destroy hard-earned winnings in a few minutes.

Build Relationships You Can Trust

This is not easy. You'll find plenty of people you can talk to in any cardroom but few you can absolutely trust to speak openly, honestly, and truthfully with you about your game. When you find these few, develop those friendships. You can discuss your play and problems with them. You will each improve as a result of reinforcing one another. But you have to be willing to give more than you get in any relationship, and a cardroom relationship is no exception.

Ask the Right Questions

Some people keep asking themselves the wrong questions. You won't learn much from asking, "Why do the bad beats always happen to me?" A question like "Why does the idiot in seat No. 5 win with aces while I always lose with them?" is self-defeating, because the very heart of these questions is based on the assumption that life at the poker table is beyond your control. *And it's not.*

If you change that assumption to one that acknowledges your own responsibility, you might ask instead: "How can I keep applying the winning strategies I've learned?" Or "What can I do to continue to prepare to win?" Perhaps a question like "How can I increase my winnings by recognizing and eliminating faults in my game?" is one you ought to contemplate asking.

If you ask yourself questions based on a model that acknowledges your own locus of control, your mind will direct itself to positive suggestions. Once you tell your mind that *you* exercise control over *your* own actions, it will suggest strategies to you based on this assumption. Contrast it with the "Why do the bad beats always happen to me?" question. Once you assume you have no control, positive answers are impossible to find.

There is always room for improvement in behavior. In fact, as the number of skilled players continues to grow, there is less of a knowledge gap between players at all levels. But some of us are going to continue to get the money, while others keep losing. It just might be that these behavioral characteristics separate consistent winners from the also-rans.

Dealing With Luck

A few years ago I used a computer to simulate 60,000 hands of $20–$40 hold'em. That's about one year of play, based on 30 hands per hour, and 2,000 hours of play (eight hours per day for 50 weeks). My objective was to determine how long it would take to get into "the long run," that elusive zone where luck is filtered out and only skill determines who wins and loses.

Since identical player programs were loaded into the computer, the long-run expectation was zero. With identical profiles each player should neither win nor lose. Each had the expectation of breaking even — in the long run.

That, however, was not the case. Overall, there were four losers and five winners. Seat No. 9 lost $3.18 per hour while seat No. 6 won at the rate of $1.99. That's a difference of more than $5 per hour — and they never got into the "long run," even after a year of simulated play.

Understanding poker's fluctuations also provides some perspective when considering your short-term results. Not only can fluctuations persist for a long time before results can be attributed solely to skill, but also there is no guarantee you will balance your books after the last hand is dealt. All probability theory offers is an equal likelihood that your results will parallel your ability.

A Lifetime of Poker

Well if a year was insufficient to get into the "long run," what about a lifetime? I asked my computer to play 3 million hands of $20–$40 hold'em. At 30 hands per hour, 2,000 hours per year, that's 50 years of poker. I don't know about you, but I'm nowhere near having played 3 million hands. Outside of the late and legendary poker stalwart Johnny Moss, I don't know anybody else who has either.

Did the results equal out over time? Not quite. After 50 simulated years, the big winner was ahead $60,214. The big loser was stuck $35,953. That's 60 cents per hour for the winner, while the big loser was stuck 35 cents per hour. All the others at the table had results somewhere in between.

Did they get into the long run? Or does the 95 cents per hour difference between the big winner and big loser mean that even a lifetime isn't sufficient to get into the long run. The answer depends upon your understanding of probability.

A Little Probability

Think about this. Suppose you were tossing coins. With a very large number of tosses, do you believe that the number of heads and tails would be exactly the same? If you do, then you would also believe that these simulated players, each programmed to play identically from a strategic perspective, ought to have identical results after 3,000,000 hands.

However, theoretical probability makes no promise to balance the books over the long haul. All theoretical probability offers is this: The coin is as likely to come down heads as tails. Not that it will, only that it is as likely to. Since there is no reason why a coin should land on one side rather than the other, they are both equally likely to happen. Still, don't expect exactly half and half — even in a large sample. While you can expect results close to theoretical probability, remember this: The coin doesn't have a memory to give it heads this time and tails the next.

If you carry this logic over to the nine computerized hold'em players, each had an equally likely chance to win. With identical playing profiles, each player's expectation was to break even. The fact that they did not break even does not negate probability theory. After all, a break-even prediction was the best forecast you could have made, and there's no way you could logically have predicted seat No. 3 would win 60 cents per hour and seat No. 1 would lose 35 cents per hour. Maybe the best you can expect over a lifetime of play is that only 1 percent to 1.5 percent of your results would be dependent on luck.

How Many Bad Players Does it Take to Make a Good Game?

In a second simulation, two poor players were substituted for two of the nine original players at the table. One played too tight. The other played too loose. I let them play for 50 years. The results: The rock lost $3 million while the loose player dropped nearly $4 million. Each of the seven other players was a lifelong winner in this game. The biggest winner was up $1.2 million. The smallest winner was ahead nearly $800,000.

Game Selection is Critical

There is a major implication here: Game selection is critical. Simply by substituting two poor players in this game of average players the big winner went from 60 cents to $12 per hour. That's a twenty-fold increase.

Game selection, according to inferences that can be drawn from these simulations, is crucial to a winning player's long-term success. Why is it so important? Every subsequent decision made at the table relates only to the hand you are involved in. (And maybe a few other hands, too, if you are setting up a move.) However, game selection has implications for every hand you choose to play — or not to play — when you are at the table. To succeed at poker you must play better than a sufficient number of your opponents to ensure that you can overcome not only their skill level, but also your cost of doing business.

Part Two:

Earning Your Degree

Whether he likes it or not, a man's character is stripped bare at the poker table; if the other players read him better than he does, he has only himself to blame. Unless he is both able and prepared to see himself as others do, flaws and all, he will be a loser in cards, as in life.

Anthony Holden: *Big Deal: A Year As A Professional Poker Player*

Chapter 4

The First Two Cards: Play Before the Flop

The Most Important Decision You'll Make

Poker is about decisions. It is, in fact, a game of decisions. While you cannot control either the way the cards fall or the actions of your opponents (although you certainly can learn to *influence* their behavior), your decisions are how you exercise your skills in a poker game.

Quality decisions separate winners from losers. When the cards have evened out in the long run, the true measure of any player's skill is the quality of decisions he made. Make better decisions and you'll win more money. Make bad decisions and you'll probably go broke. It's that simple! The better your decisions the more you can expect to win. The more erroneous your decisions, the sooner you're on the rail.

Deciding whether to see the flop with your first two cards is generally the most important decision you'll make playing hold'em. Choosing to play or toss your cards away is really a decision about investing money in a pot with the intention of winning it. It's a decision you have to make each time you're dealt a hand. So important is this decision that many experts suggest just playing correctly before the flop, at least in low-limit games, is enough to turn a loser into a break-even player, and a break-even player into a winner.

Some Decisions Are More Important Than Others

Certain decisions are more important than others, usually for one of two reasons. Some are important because you encounter them every time you play a hand — like deciding whether to see the flop. Frequency of occurrence makes these decisions critical.

Decisions are also important if they can cost you a great deal of money. Here's an example. Assume you hold the best hand after all the cards are out, but decide to call your opponent, rather than raise. While this is a bad decision, it's not an important one, since it costs you only one bet. However, if you were bet into by a habitual bluffer and mucked the best hand, that decision is important. It cost you the entire pot. In fact, if you win at a rate of two bets per hour, and that pot contained fifteen bets, it will take you an entire day's play to recoup.

Poker's Essential Decision

Every time you play poker you're confronted with this decision: Given all variables, do the cards I hold offer a positive expectation? If the answer is yes, play on. If the answer is no, wait for the next hand.

This decision is made up of many components. You must compare the odds of making the best hand with the payoff offered by the expected size of the pot. But the mathematical odds of making your hand compared with the pot odds is not all you have to consider. It's further complicated because you must also account for the game being loose or tight, passive or aggressive, with skilled or unskilled players. These elements make up the game's texture.

Here's an example. Assume you hold a reasonably good drawing hand like J–10 suited in a game with lots of raising before the flop, but not many callers. Your hand is much less valuable in that game than in one where you could expect many callers and little raising — which allows you to draw to your hand at minimal cost.

The opposite is also true. Suppose you've been dealt a pair of aces or kings, and two people call the blind before it's your turn to act. Now you must raise. You want to get more money in the pot from those who have already called. Moreover, you must try to eliminate a potential caller who might call with a hand like 9–8 suited, but wouldn't cold-call a raise for two bets. While aces or kings are an overwhelming heavy favorite against 9–8 when played heads up, the more participants in a pot, the better the chances that one of them will outdraw you.

Most players who enter a pot for one bet will call a raise when the action gets back to them. When holding a big pair, your raise will get more money in the pot from fewer players. Calling is a weak play because more opponents increase the likelihood that someone — who might not have played if he had to cold-call a raise — will get lucky.

Playing a Big Pair With a Raise in Front of You

In fact, if you hold a big pair before the flop, you should welcome a raise ahead of you. Your reraise should then eliminate all but the truest kamikazes and players holding premium hands. The secret to playing big pairs is to play them against fewer, rather than many opponents, while locking those opponents into as many bets as you can garner. If a player does call your reraise with a hand he should have thrown away, your reraise gave him that opportunity to make a mistake.

Jackpot Games Can be Different

In a jackpot game, an additional sum of money is collected each hand to fund a jackpot. The jackpot is "hit" when, in most cases, aces full or better is beaten. Both cards in each player's hand usually have to play — but there are lots of local variations. If you're uncertain, ask before you sit down. Jackpot distributions vary. Some pay 70 percent of the jackpot to the losing hand and 30 percent to the winner. Others distribute 60 percent to the loser of the hand, 20 percent to the winner, and split the remaining 20 percent among the other players seated at the table. One difference you'll probably notice in jackpot games is how tough it can be to drive opponents out before the flop. This is especially true when they hold a pair — regardless of how small it might be. Because it is tough to drive out players in a jackpot game, occasionally a player who cold-calls your raise with a small pair will flop a set and bludgeon you with it. While you'll remember when your aces or kings were crippled by a set of fours, you'll actually make more money in the long run from all the times your opponent called a double bet, didn't improve, and you won a bigger pot.

With a drawing hand, the general rule is to usually try and make your hand as cheaply as possible; however, there will be occasions when it pays to bet on the come. When you hold a premium pair, make it expensive for others to try and draw out on you. This means learning to manipulate the size of the pot by betting or raising appropriately.

Devising a preflop strategy is not as difficult as it seems, since there are a finite number of two-card holdings. But hold'em is not a game that can profitably be played by following a precise formula. To be successful, strategic concepts must be dynamic, subject to tactical adjustments as a result of position, game texture, the quality of your opponents, how they perceive and play against you, and how well you expect to play against them.

How to Play Your Starting Cards

What should you expect to find in the two cards dealt to you before the flop?

Sometimes you'll be dealt a pair. If there's no pair in your hand, the cards will be either suited or not. They also can be connected (K–Q, 8–7, 4–3). If not connected, they might be one-, two-, or three-gapped (K–J, 9–6, or 6–2). While you can make a straight with one-, two-, or three-gapped cards, the smaller the gap, the easier it is to make a straight. Suppose you hold 10-6. Your only straight possibility is 9–8–7. But if you hold 10–9, you can make a straight with K–Q–J, Q–J–8, J–8–7, and 8–7–6.

Cards that are not suited or paired, and four-gapped or larger should not be played under normal circumstances.

Since you can be dealt only 169 different two-card combinations before the flop, learning to play them is not as tough as you might think. Each possible two-card holding is shown on the chart located on the inside back cover. This color coded "Start Chart" assumes any pair is equal to any other pair of the same rank before the flop, and suited cards of the same rank have equal preflop value. For example, prior to the flop, the K♣–Q♣ is identical in value to the K♦–Q♦. But if the flop were to bring three diamonds, then the K♦–Q♦ could be priceless, and the K♣–Q♣ might be worthless and unplayable.

Once you notice that hands are arranged in descending order and are able to visualize this array without actually looking at it, it's not difficult to memorize this chart. Your mind's eye will see the deployment of playable hands from early to middle to late position.

Playable hands in early position begin with big pairs and big connectors, which fan out from the chart's upper left-hand corner. Middle- and late-position hands are tucked under the curve formed by the early-position hands, and unplayable two-card holdings are located toward the right hand side of the charts. With a little work you should be able to commit this to memory. Try visualizing it. You'll find it easier to memorize than if it were in list format.

Notice that you'll play far fewer hands in early position. You'll also find that suited cards have a lot more value than unsuited cards of equal rank. If you're new to the game, been playing indiscriminately, or have an any-two-cards-can-win philosophy, you may believe these starting requirements are too tight. To the contrary, they are somewhat loose and if you opt not to play A- J, A-10 and K- J in early position, that's OK too. And if you neglect to modify these starting hands for game conditions, you'll find them far too loose. That's important!

The strategic plan embodied in the Start Chart is not a formula to blindly follow. If the pot has been raised in front of you, you will need to tighten up significantly on the hands you play, particularly those played from early position. Let me emphasize this point. If a player who acts before you has raised, you need to tighten up significantly, and throw away many of the hands you'd play if the pot had not been raised.

Sklansky's Card Rankings

Hold'em Poker by David Sklansky first presented groupings of two-card holdings that the author advocated playing in early, middle, and late position. These recommendations were modified slightly in *Hold'em Poker For Advanced Players* by David Sklansky and Mason Malmuth. Start Chart offers a minor departure from the groupings recommended by Sklansky and Malmuth. The major difference lies in the presentation. By displaying starting hands graphically, I find them easier to commit to memory than if they were displayed in list form.

I also recommend that every serious player read Sklansky's and Malmuth's books. So comprehensive are they, that players who do not acquire and study those two texts will not advance nearly as far as they should. Worse yet, they could be left behind.

Modifying Your Strategy in Early Position

Hold'em is a complex game, and you can't play your first two cards mechanically. Consider a hand like 10–9 suited. Just because it is a playable early-position hand in a normal game doesn't mean you must play it. In a game with frequent preflop raising and short-handed pots, it is often unplayable. Yes, you might flop a monster hand with it, and when you do you'll gain all those extra bets resulting from those preflop raises. But it is simply not the kind of hand you're going to flop a monster with all that often. It is a very speculative hand — one better played inexpensively and from late position. Ideally, you'd want to play this kind of hand on the button, when you're last to act and there are seven or eight callers in an unraised pot ahead of you. Now you can take a shot and toss your hand away if the flop doesn't help you.

Here's another example. Assume you hold a "playable" hand like K-J before the flop, but the pot has been raised in front of you.

What should you do? Most of the time you should throw it away. Chances are the raiser holds better cards than yours. Not only are you an underdog in this situation, but even if the flop contains a king or a jack, you can't be sure you have the best hand.

Be Selective

Absolutely essential to your success as a player is the discipline to be very selective about the hands you play. In fact, a quick way to go broke is to play every hand. Yes, you'll win more pots along your personal road to ruin, but your objective is to win the most money, not the most pots.

Still, in a typical game with four or five active players before the flop with little raising, you can play hands like 10-9 suited. But if you're in a very tight game, where there are typically only one or two callers, this is not a hand you'd want to play too often. Here's why. Assume you call, along with one other player, plus the big blind. Chances are you will not have the best hand after the flop. In situations where the flop helps no one, you do not stand a very good chance of winning. Suppose the blind held a Q-5, unsuited. A real rag? Sure. But having gotten a free play in the unraised pot, the blind's high card will go on to win if the turn and river cards are also blanks.

Be Aggressive!

This raises another interesting point. If calling was wrong, what about raising? Under the right circumstances it's a good idea. If you are in late position and no one has called the blinds, raising with a hand such as 10-9 suited is usually better than calling. But not from an early position, since you don't know the quality of your opponents' hands, and they have yet to act. Someone with a big pair, or bigger connectors, could reraise. Then you're trapped for three bets before the flop, and you're an underdog to boot. The point, once again, is to be very selective with the hands you play. In fact, a hand like 10-9 is one I'll usually throw away in early position, but under the right circumstances, I'll raise with it in late position.

Complex Situations in Early Position

Complex situations arise whenever you are confronted with a decision that might move you off the starting requirements shown on the Start Chart. Because complex situations, by definition, are tough to resolve, their frequency speaks volumes about the kind of game you're in. If you regularly have to make choices you're not sure about, consider changing tables or packing it in until the tough players leave and the game becomes softer.

Complex situations stem from uncertainty over how to play your own hand, or respond to an action by your opponent. What should you do, for example, when you're dealt a medium or big pair in early position? If your big pair is aces, kings, or queens, you should raise — or reraise if the pot was raised in front of you. If you're the first one in, raise with any pair of tens or higher, and occasionally — to add some deception to your game — raise with any pair of sevens or higher.

With a small pair, you're better off either heads up — in which case you're hoping your opponent is holding big cards — or against a large field. When you're playing a small pair against a large field, you're hoping to flop three-of-a-kind. If you're up against a large number of opponents, any overcards on the board are going to give someone a better hand than yours.

Worse yet, if you hold a pair of sevens or eights, and they are higher than any of the cards appearing on the flop, the board itself will be so tightly clustered that a straight or straight draw is usually a strong possibility. With many players in the pot, this must be reckoned with in your subsequent decisions. Both of these scenarios can be quite complex, and in higher limit games, tough, tricky players may seize these opportunities to drive you off the pot. But if you're playing in lower limit games, where you typically find many opponents taking the flop, the need for trickery is minimized. Since there are so many callers, you generally have to show down the best hand to win.

Playing Medium Pairs

With a medium pair, you might have to flop a set to win the pot. If I'm holding a pair of kings, only an ace on the flop may give someone a bigger pair. If you hold tens, every face card on the board creates a potential pair bigger than yours. If you don't flop a set or overpair, it is difficult to justify continuing with your hand, particularly when two face cards fall on the flop and there is multiway action.

Here's an example. Suppose you're dealt a pair of tens in early position and there are four callers. The flop is A-J-6, all of mixed suits. Since most of your opponents will play big cards, chances are one of them has paired an ace or a jack, especially if there is a bet and call before the action reaches you. While there are players who will ride a pair of tens to the end of the track against similar flops, they will throw off a bundle of money in the process.

Under complex conditions, you often need to think more about your opponents than your hand. Ask yourself this: What kind of hands would they be playing? Sure, one of them might have called with K-Q, or 9-8 suited, but it is also likely that someone holds an ace or jack. If so, you're now a big underdog, as only two of the remaining 47 cards will help you. Investing money in this pot is a poor investment, because the pot odds will never offset the mathematical odds against making your hand. People who continue to play under such circumstances will lose money — lots of it.

Advanced players always ask themselves, "What does my opponent think I'm playing?" The ability to get into your opponent's head is a rare skill — one that really separates great players from all the others. As a beginner, this is not a skill you'll master easily, or immediately. For now, just be aware of this ability; you'll cultivate it with experience.

Playing Smaller Pairs

With smaller pairs, unless you are up against only one other player, you usually have to flop a set to make it worth your while to stay in the hand. If you don't flop a set when dealt a pair of deuces, for example, you can be certain that every subsequent card will be an overcard. The only way you could win is for the board to miss everyone — and with multiway action, that's unlikely.

Most expert players routinely throw away small pairs — unless they can play them against many opponents without risking a raise. In jackpot games, many of your opponents will always see the flop with any pair, no matter how many preflop raises they have to call. Because of this, you'll find yourself up against small sets more frequently.

When you have a big pair, or make two pair, and get beaten by a small set, it's frustrating. However, you'll make up for some of it on those occasions when you make a full house, a straight or a flush against an opponent who shouldn't have been there in the first place. Now you'll get all the action you want and you'll love it.

Disadvantages of Early Position

A major disadvantage of early position is having to act first on each successive round of betting. Consequently, speculative hands such as smaller, suited connectors, and even small pairs, are risky. It is preferable to play these hands as cheaply as possible against a large number of opponents. If you're in early position you have no way of knowing how many others will contest the pot, or whether it will be raised. As a result, these hands are better played from the rear. Playing them early risks a raise behind you. This makes it more expensive for you to play these holdings. If there is a raise, you may not attract the number of callers you want to ensure a nice payoff on those occasions when you make a big hand.

To play smaller suited connectors effectively in early position, you should be in a game where preflop raises are infrequent. If you continue to play hands like this in tight games (with few opponents in each pot) or aggressive games with frequent raising, it will prove costly.

Good Early Position Hands

Hands that do well in early position are big pairs, medium pairs that can either improve to a set or survive as an overpair after the flop, and big connectors — preferably suited. No matter how big the connectors may be, you have to be willing to release them when warranted. For example, A♣–K♣ is a big underdog against a flop like 10–10–9, especially if that flop contains two suited cards (other than clubs). Some players never release an A–K, no matter how badly the flop misses them. This is a major leak in their game. You might fall in love with A–K, but you don't have to marry it.

Just because a hand is playable in early position does not mean it is playable all the way to the river. Hand values often change dramatically once the flop hits the board, and when this happens you must be willing to release hands that held promise before the flop.

The key to successful early-position play is selectivity. Base that selectivity on the playable hands shown on the Start Chart, but be prepared to limit the number of hands you play when the game is very tight, overly aggressive, or both. If the game is very tight, however, you can steal some pots from early position. Nevertheless, most low-limit games are anything but overly tight, so if you plan on bluffing up front in an attempt to steal the blinds, be forewarned, and be careful.

Middle-Position Play and Late-Position Play

Having been cautioned about early-position play, "What," you might ask, "can you do differently in middle or late position?"

You can open up a bit more. The later you act, the more information you have about your opponents' hands and there's less chance you will face a raise, since fewer players remain to act after you. Not only can you play more hands in late position, you can play them more creatively.

Suppose you've been dealt

in eighth position and no one has called the blind by the time it's your turn to act. You'd routinely throw this hand away in early or middle position. But with only the blinds active, go ahead and raise. If the blinds hold trash hands, they'll probably throw their cards away — even if they suspect you're on a steal. If they call and an ace falls, you still stand a good chance of having the best hand. If the board doesn't help anyone, your lone ace will win the pot.

But that doesn't mean you can play any two cards, or even all the playable hands on the Start Chart, in all circumstances. Suppose you're dealt

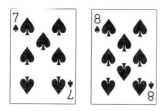

on the button. The player in position No. 4 raises, and gets two cold calls by the time it's your turn to act. What should you do? Simple. Ask yourself, "What's the worst hand my opponent would raise with in fourth position," and "What's the worst hand other opponents would call with?" Regardless of how much you might like to play that 8♠–7♠, you cannot logically conclude that the raiser and both callers are playing hands of less value than yours. Chances are you're already beaten in three places. Toss your hand away. However, another couple of players would justify a call because the pot might get quite large, even if you knew you were up against an overpair.

If you call, you'll need to flop either two pair, a flush, or a straight to bet out on the flop, and typically either a flush or straight draw to call an opponent's bet on the flop. However, even if you flop the bottom pair, you should call the bet if the pot is large enough to warrant it. If one or more face cards flop, you have to credit at least one of your three opponents with a big pair. If they bet and you call, you're an underdog. You may be up against a bigger pair, two pair, or a set. Even if you flop a flush draw, you won't know for certain that your opponent isn't holding two suited connectors larger than yours. If you're unfortunate enough to get into that matchup and make your flush, here's what will happen. He'll bet, you'll raise, and he will reraise you. Now you're trapped and likely to call him down to the river — only to find yourself losing a stack of chips along the way.

Thinking About Your Opponent's Hand

The lesson to be learned from these examples is that you must always be extremely selective, even after you've chosen to play a hand aggressively. When you've been raised, force yourself to answer this question, "What's my opponent likely to be raising with?" Many beginning hold'em players simply do not play their opponents' hands. Making the mistake of playing only your hand is a common, costly error among beginners and many low-limit players.

Remember, hold'em is not like video poker, where you need to make certain hands of absolute value to win. You only need to make a hand better than your opponent's when both are shown down at the river. Sometimes a mere pair may be sufficient to take the pot, while at other times big hands like sets, straights, and flushes will lose. Often the probabilities of better hands can be deduced through a combination of reading the board and analyzing your opponents' betting patterns. But this is not foolproof, and you won't always know for certain. Occasionally you'll lay down the best hand to a bluff. Nevertheless, it is much more costly to carelessly throw more money into a pot you're unlikely to win simply because you neglected to heed those warning signs along the way.

Playing Small Pairs in Late Position

Smaller pairs become playable in later positions, unless there has been a raise in front of you. With smaller pairs, you're hoping for a lot of opponents plus you want to flop a set. When you get lucky and make that set, you're positioned to win a large pot.

How you play your set depends on the texture of the game. If the board does not appear threatening and you're up against aggressive opponents who like to jam the pot, go ahead and meekly call, until the turn — when you'll get an opportunity to fire in a raise. When the board is threatening, you might want to come out betting or raise an earlier bettor when it's your turn to act. Even if your opponent makes an apparent straight or flush on the turn, you're still getting good pot odds on your chances of improving to a full house or better if the board pairs. Go ahead and keep calling until you make your hand. Then raise.

If you don't flop a set or a straight draw, your small pair will simply not stand up and should be abandoned if someone bets the flop.

Here's an exception. Suppose you called with 6–6 and the flop is 7–5–4 of mixed suits. Although you didn't make a set, you flopped an open-end straight draw and can continue playing. If a six were to come on the turn, you'd now have three sixes, but there's a good chance one of your opponents made a straight. If the board pairs on the river, however, then your full house is a big favorite to win the pot.

Playing Big Pairs

When dealt a big pair, you should raise before the flop. Your objectives are to limit the number of players, while hoping your big pair will be sufficient to capture the pot without improvement, and to give your opponents a chance to make the mistake of calling your bet when the odds don't warrant it. If you get a lot of callers, you'll need to reassess whether or not your pair is still the best hand. For example, a flop like Q–J–5 is much more likely to give someone two pair than a flop like Q–6–2. Why? Because many of your opponents will play a hand like Q–J. They won't play Q–6 or 6–2.

Playing a Big Pair Against Many Opponents

Playing a single big pair against four, five, or six opponents takes the kind of judgment you'll acquire only after extensive playing experience. It's tough to release a big pair. All good players will, when conditions warrant, toss a good hand away. Players who will not release aces, kings, or queens lose more money than they should. Although you cannot prevent yourself from being out-played and releasing the best hand on occasion, the money you save from the losing bet you don't make is just as valuable as money won.

I'm certainly not suggesting passive play. Far from it. I recommend aggressive play, tempered with selectivity. Selectivity means not only tossing away weak starting hands, but also releasing medium strength hands when you know you are beaten. Let someone else call to keep 'em honest. When you know you're beaten or when the pot odds don't justify it, toss your hand away.

How to Play Smaller Connectors

Playing smaller connectors, whether suited or not, is a simple proposition. Think of them as bargain basement hands — to be played only in unraised pots and against lots of opponents. When you take the flop with small connectors, you're hoping to flop a big hand and trap as many opponents as you can. This won't happen very often, but when it does, you should win a big pot. If you're not prepared to release smaller connectors when you don't hit your hand, however, you will pay dearly. In fact, if you can't bring yourself to release hands like these, you'd be better off tightening up your starting requirements by never playing them at all.

Sometimes you'll face difficult decisions with these hands. Suppose you call with a 7–6 suited on the button against five opponents. The flop is K–7–4. The blinds and one other opponent check, and the player to your right bets. What should you do? Do you call with second-best pair? Do you automatically put the bettor on a pair of kings and release your hand? Could your opponent be on a steal since there were no bettors in front of him?

What about the blinds and the other active opponent? Did the flop miss all of them? Or is one of them sandbagging — hoping to get in a check–raise on fourth street when the betting limits double? Do you raise, representing a big hand, hoping to win the pot right there?

These are not easy decisions. The correct play, which is partially dependent on the size of the pot, also hinges on knowing your opponents and how they play. These situations require a good deal of playing experience, and if you're unsure of what to do, I'd suggest you err on the side of caution.

Selectivity — The Key to Preflop Play

The key to successful preflop play in hold'em is selectivity — putting yourself in positions offering favorable pot odds. When you're in a favorable spot, you need to be aggressive, either to get more money in the pot when you have a big hand or to eliminate competition when you're holding the kind of hand that plays best against fewer opponents.

In hold'em, as in all forms of poker, you do not want to make the second-best hand, especially when you don't realize you're beaten. Recognizing you're beaten, even when you hold a big hand, takes knowledge and experience.

Underlying all strategic ideas is the need to be a selective, aggressive, and disciplined player. While all the theory you'll need to become a skilled hold'em player is available in this book, discipline is not. You'll have to apply it on your own. If you're able to exercise discipline 100 percent of the time, you can look forward to a bright future at the tables.

Chapter 5

R egardless of one's creativity, it's hard to paint well without mastering brush techniques. James Joyce didn't start out writing in streams of consciousness before first mastering the art of story telling. And even someone as precocious at Mozart, who wrote symphonies before he was ten years old, didn't begin there. He just evolved more quickly than most. By the same token, one won't win at Texas hold'em either — or any form of poker for that matter — without first developing a solid set of starting standards.

There's not a poker pundit worth his salt who wouldn't advise adopting a solid set of standards as a guide to determining when, and under what circumstances, to enter a hand. David Sklansky was a pioneer, developing and promulgating Texas hold'em starting standards more than twenty years ago. While he's modified those standards over the years, they've held up remarkably well, and learning his "hand categories" has given many beginning players a sense of confidence they might otherwise have lacked.

My starting standards do not differ much from those developed by Sklansky. By presenting them graphically rather than in a list or groupings, I hoped that the visual nature of their depiction would permit anyone to study the chart, close his or her eyes, and visualize the array of hands — thus enabling players to learn starting standards without the necessity for rote memorization.

The desire to eliminate the need for memorizing starting standards also led to a unique effort by Berkeley mathematician and poker whiz William Chen. Bill posted his "power ratings" to the Internet newsgroup, rec.gambling.poker. Chen began his post by saying: "OK! No more need to memorize which hands belong in various categories." Chen's idea came about after discussing a column in *Card Player* magazine I wrote about starting hands. "The question," according to Chen, "is whether we can limit the amount of memorization needed, and maybe even give some intuition about the game."

Here is Bill Chen's formula for developing power ratings for hold'em hands. Look at your hand. You're going to "score" it by giving yourself points for your highest card, according to the following charts:

Highest Card	
Ace	10 points
King	8 points
Queen	7 points
Jack	6 points
10 through 2	half of face value
	(10 = 5 points, 9 = 4.5 points)

Pairs
•   multiply the pair by 2
•   minimum points for a pair is 5 points (deuces through fives)

Suited
•   add 2 points for suited cards

Gaps and Connectors
•   Subtract one point for one-gappers (AQ, J9)
•   Subtract two points for two-gappers (AJ, J8)
•   Subtract four points for four-gappers (J7, 73)
•   Subtract five points for bigger gaps, including A2, A3, and A4.
•   Give yourself one extra point if your cards are connected, or one-gapped and your highest card is lower than a queen, since that allows you to make all the higher straights.

Here are some examples of power ratings, using Bill Chen's method.

AA = 20 points (2 x 10 points)

AKs = 12 points (10 points for the ace, + 2 points because they are suited)

J9 = 6 points (6 points for the jack – 1 point because they are gapped + 1 point for the "straight" bonus)

If you take the time to work it out, you'll find these power ratings for hold'em starting hands.

Hand Power Rankings	
20 points	AA
16 points	KK
14 points	QQ
12 points	JJ, AKs
11 points	AQs
10 points	TT, AK, AJs, KQs
9 points	99, AQ, KJs, QJs, JTs
8 points	88, AJ, ATs, KQ, KTs, QTs, J9s, T9s
7.5 points	98s
7 points	77, KJ, QJ, JT, Axs, Q9s, T8s, 87s,
6.5 points	97s, 76s
6 points	66, 55, AT, KT, QT, J9, T9, K9s, J8s, 86s, 65s
5.5 points	98, 75s, 54s
5 points	44, 33, 22, Kxs, Ax, Q9, T8, 87, Q8s, T7s, 64s, 43s

Chen reminds us that the "…hand rankings only tell you which hands to play, and not whether to come in for a raise." He mentions that he would play hands with a power ranking of eight points or higher under the gun, seven points or higher in middle position, six points in late position, and 5.5 points on the button. Whether you should adopt his suggestions for whether or not to play depends, of course, on the relative aggressiveness of the game you're in, and the skill of your opponents.

Chen also recommends having a hand worth at least 10 points to come in cold after an early raise, or nine points against a "typical" player. He also recommends isolating a raiser by three-betting anytime you intend to take a pair up against him. He goes on to point out that he thinks it "…a good rule that each raise pushes up the requirements by at least two points."

To come in cold after a reraise, Chen recommends at least a twelve-point hand. He would defend his big blind with any hand rated 5.5 points or higher, although he freely admits that's he's been told he defends his big blind too liberally. If the small blind is less than half of the big blind, he recommends using the guidelines for calling a raise, but if the small blind is half the big blind or more, he recommends loosening the raise-calling requirements by a point. If there were no raise, he'll usually call from the small blind with five or more points.

Chen's power-ratings differ somewhat from Sklansky's hand rankings and from my own, which were derived heuristically, and are not formulaic in origin like Chen's rankings. But that's not the point. We are all going down the same path in the same general direction, and the fact that one could argue the night away about which method lies closer to theoretical perfection is simply a waste of time. What is important is that anyone aspiring to become a solid hold'em player needs to have some starting standards to guide his or her play.

If it is easier to memorize hand groupings, then Sklansky's hand values are for you. If you are visually oriented, and can close your eyes and recall a pictorial array that you've just seen, then my starting hand chart will lead you in the right direction.

But if you are computational in your approach to poker, then Dr. William Chen's power ranking method of deriving starting hands might be just the thing for you. Regardless of the approach you elect to follow, you will be far ahead of anyone who decides which cards to play on whim, or instinct, or by his internal vision of how the cards are running that day.

The biggest stride forward you will make as a hold'em player will not come from polishing your starting standards down to a perfect sheen, but from adopting reasonable standards in the first place. Without them, you will be lost. And any refinement made once you've integrated them into your game is merely fine-tuning.

F or hold'em players the blinds are as unavoidable as death, taxes, and bad beats — just a consequence of life at the poker table. How you play the blinds, however, will have a large bearing on your success at the game.

When the Pot Has Not Been Raised

If you're in the big blind in an unraised pot, consider yourself fortunate. You've gotten to see the flop for free. You might just flop a huge hand with two cards you otherwise would not have played. When you're in the small blind, you can see the flop for half a bet — or in games structured like the $15–$30 games in Southern California, where the blinds are $15 and $10 — you can see the flop for one-third of a bet.

Seeing the flop at a bargain-basement price somewhat compensates for having to act first on each succeeding round of betting. In a game where the small blind is one-half the big blind, you can see the flop in unraised pots with hands like 7-6 offsuit.

While you're going to be disappointed with the flop the majority of the time, it's great to flop a big hand in the blind (two pair or better) and end up winning a nice pot.

Even when you are able to see the flop for free, you will surrender your hand most of the time when someone bets.

Holding a Big Hand in the Blind

Every so often you'll be dealt a pair of aces, kings or queens, or an A–K in the blind. There are some players who automatically raise with these hands, regardless of any previous action. Players who routinely do this give their opponents too much evidence. By raising from the blind, you are announcing to your opponents that you have an exceptional hand. Not just a good hand, a great one.

Suppose you called from late position with a 9-8 suited, and you are raised by the big blind. You'll take the flop planning to continue only if it is very favorable to you and unfavorable to your opponent.

Now the flop comes 9–8–4. You've got two pair, and your opponent in the blind — whose raise was a ringing exclamation that he's likely to be holding a very big pair — is forced to act *first* on each betting round.

With a big pair, he's not afraid of the board and will probably bet. You can call him on the flop. And if a safe card falls, you can raise him on the turn. Tied to a big pair, most players in low- to mid-limit games are not going to release aces or kings when they're raised. It will be a crying call, but they'll call the turn. They'll check the river. And even when positive they're beaten, they'll call your bet.

Most low- to mid-limit players will not release a big pair unless the board overtly shouts "straight" or "flush," and there is a bet and a raise in front of them. Take advantage of this tendency by check-raising your opponent from the blind when you know he plans to bet a hand you can beat.

If your opponent simply *checks* a big hand in the blind, you will not have any idea about his holdings. Since he got a free play in the blind, he could have anything. A 7–2 offsuit is as likely as an A–K, and a meager pair of deuces is as probable as aces. In fact, if he's holding a big pair, and fortunate enough to flop a set, he can check the turn anticipating that one of his opponents will bet — allowing him to check-raise with the certainty that he holds the best hand.

Even when the flop is very unfavorable, if you didn't raise with your big pair in the blind, you should find it easier to release your hand. Let's say you're holding a pair of black aces in the big blind and the flop contains three hearts. You'll probably check and call on the flop, and check again on the turn. If there's a bet and raise, your aces are more easily abandoned when you don't commit yourself to them by raising from the blind.

Marginal Hands in the Blind

Most of the time you'll be dealt marginal hands in the blind. If you're in the big blind, and there is no raise in front of you, simply check when it's your turn to act and wish for a favorable flop. If there is a raise, you're confronted with whether to call or toss your hand away.

Most players in low- to mid-limit games defend their blinds too often. You simply can't call a raise with a hand like 8–5, even if that raise represents only half a bet to you. On the other hand, if you're holding a hand like K–2 suited, and there are four or five callers before it is raised, you should call. Unless you flop two pair, trips, or a four-flush or better, you will have to release your hand if one of your opponents bets into the flop. In essence, what you're doing is calling because you're getting high implied odds with the kind of cards that can improve to a big hand. If you happen to hit your hand, your opponents probably won't suspect its strength until too late.

When you're in the small blind, you need an even stronger hand to call a raise, since it will cost you more than half a bet. In most games it will cost you a bet and a half to call a raise from the small blind. In games structured like the $15–$30 the cost is a bet and a third.

Considerations in the Small Blind

In the small blind you have another consideration — whether to call for that fraction of a bet when the pot is not raised. In small- and mid-limit games, most players will call in the small blind with almost any hand. Even though it costs only a half bet to call from the small blind when the pot hasn't been raised, you still shouldn't call with just any hand. Unless you have a really good hand — the kind that plays well from early position — you need to limit your calls to hands that offer potential for improvement. You should also avoid playing hands that can improve to second best.

While hands like 7–2 and 9–3 are basically unplayable even when they cost only half a bet, hands like 7–6 suited — which can improve to a flush or straight with a favorable flop — should be played from the small blind in unraised pots. This is particularly true when it is a multiway pot, since the hand — with its flush and straight potential — plays better against a large field.

If you're playing in a game where the small blind is two-thirds of the big blind, you can play just about any hand from the small blind in an unraised pot. Because the cost is only one-third of a bet, you can take the long odds with a 9–3, and hope to flop something like K–9–3. Just be prepared to throw most of your hands away after the flop. If you flop one pair, it probably won't be the top pair, plus your kicker is weak. You must get away from hands like these or you'll throw off a lot of money calling bigger hands that are overwhelming favorites.

In fact, if you find it difficult to release such hands, you will need to tighten your standards in the blind and only play big cards that figure to be a favorite if the flop hits them.

Raising in the Small Blind

If you're dealt a big pair or an A–K in the small blind, and there are not many callers, a raise might prevent the big blind from playing, unless he also has a very good hand. Any rational player respects a raise from the small blind.

Since big pairs play better against a small field of opponents, your raise should limit your opposition and place more money in the pot. When you're in the blind, you're usually better off playing against a small field, especially since you have the added disadvantage of acting first on each succeeding betting round.

If you're in the small blind and only one opponent called from late position, you can occasionally raise regardless of what you're holding. If any big cards flop, your bet stands a good chance of eliminating your opponent. Since your opponent only called from late position, it's difficult to credit him with big cards. More than likely he's holding something like 8–7. Heads up, and facing a flop with overcards, he's likely to fold in the face of a bet.

This is not a tactic you can employ routinely. Anyone who is observant will simply take note of your behavior and soon begin reraising you.

Summary

- Most of the time when you're in the blind and encounter a raise you're going to throw your hand away.

- Only play your better hands for half a bet, but play most of your hands when the cost is only one-third of a bet.

- Most of the time the flop will be unfavorable to you, and once someone bets, you'll wind up tossing your hand away.

- If the flop is favorable, you still have the disadvantage of acting first on each succeeding round of betting.

- The best, and most succinct advice anyone can offer about playing in the blind is to play very few hands — and play them cautiously.

Chapter 7

Playing Big Slick

Big Slick

When it comes to big hands, all of us want to be dealt A–A or K–K. The reality is that we'll be dealt A–K more frequently. In recent years there has been some debate over how to play A–K, or *Big Slick* as it's called by most hold'em players. Exploring both sides of this debate will expose you to some strategic thinking you can use to assess other poker hands in addition to this one.

Conventional wisdom says that when you're dealt A–K you do one thing with it: Raise. While some players just call occasionally to incorporate some deception into their game, most play Big Slick as fast as a pair of aces or kings.

To many players it is a power-raising hand. You're dealt Big Slick and there's a raise in front of you? No problem. Reraise.

What if you raise then flop three rags? No problem when you're holding Big Slick. Come out betting on the flop and bet again on the turn. Conventional wisdom holds that if the flop doesn't hit anybody, your preflop raise and subsequent bets will probably drive out all but the truest of kamikazes. Your raise may even limit the number of players so that you have a reasonable chance of winning even if you don't flop anything, and if that's the case you ought to raise most of the time.

Is Conventional Wisdom Correct?

But is conventional wisdom correct? Just because it's "conventional" doesn't make it so. Remember, conventional wisdom used to state the earth was flat. In his *Caro's 12 Days to Hold'em Success Report*, poker authority Mike Caro expressed the opinion that you're usually better off calling with Big Slick, taking the flop, and seeing what develops.

If Caro's opinion is correct and conventional wisdom — still gospel to the vast majority of limit hold'em players — isn't, then substantial profit opportunities are available by exploiting incorrect strategies and employing correct ones.

To shed some more light on this murky subject, let's begin by examining why you might raise or call with Big Slick.

Assume there are four or five players who have already called the big blind and you're in one of the later positions. It may seem obvious, but it's important to recognize that when you raise in late position, you're doing so to get more money in the pot. When you're a late raiser and there are already a lot of callers, you're not going to thin out the field. While you may knock out the blinds, the other players who called the original bet will usually call your raise.

By raising in this position you're representing a big hand. If the flop contains an ace or king, you're probably in the lead. However, if the flop contains one of your cards and two or three sequenced or suited cards, you could very well be in trouble.

What do you do now? To bet or not to bet, that is the question. A bet should eliminate anyone the flop hasn't helped, but it certainly won't chase out someone who is drawing to a better hand than yours. If the board is three-sequenced or suited, one of your opponents may already have made his hand, and is simply waiting until the turn to check-raise.

Moreover, if you power-raised before the flop, a player holding second or bottom pair who called your initial raise (and now has two bets invested) may now be wed to a hand he might have otherwise tossed away. Thus committed, there is always the chance he will draw out on you by making trips or two pair on the turn or the river.

What About Limping In With A–K?

If you quietly *limp in* from late position with Big Slick, you've given no clues about the quality of your hand. While this doesn't get any more money into the pot and allows weaker hands to play against you, it provides plenty of deception when the flop is favorable.

Anytime the flop contains an ace or a king, you have to assume you're in the lead, particularly if you're up against only one (or even both) of the blinds. If the flop is *ragged* (no face cards, mixed suits, and full of gaps), however, you'll simply never know where you are relative to the blinds. Since the blinds, in an unraised pot, can be holding anything, they are just as likely to be helped by a flop containing three rags as three big cards. This is particularly true for the big blind, who is getting a *free play* in an unraised pot. If rags flop and one of the blinds bets, you can toss your hand away unless you suspect your opponent of bluffing.

The logic behind just calling with Big Slick is this: Although a powerful holding, A–K is still a drawing hand. Given the fact that most of the time you're probably not going to like the flop, it is cheaper to see the flop and play appropriately from there. Why is the flop so critical? Simple. Before the flop you've seen only two cards. After the flop more than 70 percent of your hand has been defined.

If you're in the kind of game where players routinely limp in with hands like A–5 or K–9 and subsequently bet out if an ace or king flops, you are in a position to raise them because you only *called* with Big Slick. Had you raised before the flop, those same players who limped in with no-kicker hands (a hand containing an ace with a small side card, or kicker, such as A-8) would probably not come out betting when a big card flopped — since they are likely to fear that the raiser has top pair with a better kicker.

Yet if everyone stopped raising before the flop with Big Slick, and simply limped in, the deception factor associated with making that play would be lost. But as long as players routinely raise with Big Slick, you can incorporate some deception into your game by limping in, taking the flop, then speeding up when the flop proves favorable.

Reasons to Raise With Big Slick

Why fire in a power raise with Big Slick, since by doing so you're announcing that you have a big hand? Here's the conventional wisdom side of the debate. If you raise with Big Slick and you're able to thin the field, you can generally take control of the play on the flop. If the flop, for example, comes Q–7–4 and one of the blinds checks with a hand like 4–5, your bet might cause him to fold the best hand. Because you raised before the flop, he has to put you on something. You could have raised with a pair of 10s through aces — as well as with A–K. If you had raised with a big pair or a hand like A–Q or K–Q, your opponent is a real longshot to draw out on you.

When you examine the flop and are trying to determine if it helped anyone, you need to be very aware of the game's texture. If, for example, you're playing in a game where there are typically very few callers and you suddenly find yourself in a pot with six- or seven-way action, you can assume your A–K is up against some quality draws (J–Q suited or mid-sized pairs). But if you're dealt Big Slick in a game where nearly every pot has six callers, the calling hands are likely to be weaker. You can probably expect to see hands like K–9, A–8, or worse at the showdown. When you're in a game like this and make two pair, you are hoping that your opponents also make two pair. If the board shows A–K–8 when you're holding Big Slick and your opponent has A–8, you'll get all the action you want — and you're gonna love it!

How Should You Play Big Slick?

Now that you've seen both sides of the argument, what should you do? Do you raise with Big Slick or simply limp in? Do you try to take control of the hand on the flop — regardless of what might fall — or quietly call while simultaneously setting yourself up to raise your opponents if the flop is favorable to you? How should you play it?

I find some merit in each of these somewhat conflicting strategies. My own inclination is to limp-in with Big Slick if I'm in late position and three or more players have called the blinds in front of me. With four players already active, I'm going to assume the flop will help someone. If that someone is me, I'm going to raise anybody who comes out betting on the flop — unless, of course, the board is three-sequenced or three-suited. In that case, I'll just call if my ace gives me four to the nut-flush draw and hope to raise on the turn or river. If I've got the wrong ace, I may raise anyway to try to get heads up with the bettor and steal it on the turn. If I don't raise, I'm usually going to toss my hand away.

On the other hand, if only the blinds are active, or if I'm up against the blinds and only one caller, I'll usually raise. If the flop is favorable, I will have gotten more money in the pot. If I miss the flop, I still have an opportunity to bet out and steal the pot. In this case, I'll usually play the same way regardless of whether my hand is suited or not.

Two diametrically-opposed strategic approaches to the same hand leads to the obvious question: Which one is correct? I'm not altogether certain, but I believe that conventional wisdom is correct *most of the time*. Nevertheless, the choice of which strategy to employ depends in part on the texture of the game, how many aggressive players are at the table, and how much control you can exert over your opponents when you raise.

While I see merit on both sides and my own inclination leans in the direction of the conventional wisdom, I believe many of my opponents overplay A–K. They see Big Slick as a premium hand. I see it as a premium *drawing hand*. Because of my opinion, I don't put it in the must-raise category. I also believe a mixed strategy is appropriate — sometimes calling, sometimes raising — again depending on position, the number of active players, when it's your turn to act, and the texture of the game.

Chapter 8

The Flop: A Defining Moment

"Defining Moments" are crystallized instants in time, forever frozen in memory, imprinted into consciousness, never to be forgotten. Like Armstrong walking on the moon, JFK's assassination, or the first home run you hit in little league, these moments of experience shape the way you perceive and value the world around you.

Hold'em, like life itself, has its defining moment. It's the flop — the critical time in each hand you play. Unlike seven-card stud, where cards that follow your initial holding are parceled out one by one with a round of betting after each, when you see the flop in hold'em, you're looking at five-sevenths of your hand. That's 71 percent of your hand, and the cost is only a single round of betting.

Because betting limits increase on the turn and river, the flop is even more of a bargain. In a $3–$6 hold'em game, you can often see the flop for $3. Future betting, if there are no raises, would cost you $3 on the flop (the cost to see the turn card), $6 on the turn (the price to look at the river card), and $6 on the river (the final round of betting after all the cards are out), for a total of $15 dollars more. Look at it this way: *The flop is a bargain.* You can see 71 percent of your hand for 17 percent of its potential cost. But don't get carried away by the relationship between the cost of the flop and the price of the rest of the hand. You can't play any two starting cards just because the cost of the flop is relatively low. The flop is a only a bargain as long as your two starting cards warrant seeing it.

The implication should be abundantly clear. If the flop does not fit your hand, you ought to be done with it — unless there are some very solid reasons to stick around. In Chapter Four you were urged to be very selective about which hands you play before the flop. You also have to be selective about those hands you continue with after the flop. Playing longshot holdings is a sure way to go broke, unless, of course, you're getting huge pot odds to call. Why? Because, after the flop, the relationship between the betting and the cards to come is reversed. Now you're looking at spending 83 percent of the potential cost of a hand for the remaining 29 percent of the cards!

Fit or fold. That's the concept. Fit can take one of three forms: (1) The flop fits because it improves your hand; (2) it offers a draw that figures to pay off handsomely if you hit it; (3) or you already hold a pair higher than the biggest card that flops.

Fit or fold. If you don't improve to a big hand or a draw with a potential payoff exceeding the odds against making your hand, get out — and do it fast! Many beginners, as well as experienced low-limit players, often stick around for one more card. This is a major flaw in their game. In fact, if you play winning poker under all other circumstances, this single flaw is critical enough to turn a winner into a lifelong loser! When the flop doesn't fit your hand — and that's going to happen about two-thirds of the time — you must release it unless the odds offered by the pot exceed the odds against making your hand, or you have reason to believe you can steal the pot by bluffing.

Flops You're Going to Love

While you're not going to like the flop most of the time, there are those rare instances when it fits like a tailor-made suit. When you're fortunate enough to flop a straight flush, four-of-a-kind, a full house, or the nut flush, your major concern is not whether you'll win, but how much money you can extract from your opponents.

While a straight flush or quads are usually unbeatable, you can fill up and still lose to a bigger full house or a bigger four-of-a-kind. Occasionally you'll flop a flush, only to have someone else flop a set and run you down when the turn or river card pairs the board to make a full house.

But with flops like these, look at the bright side. What should you do when you've got a monster hand? Your first order of business is to examine the texture of the flop. Based on the betting pattern prior to the flop, try to determine whether one or more of your opponents has made a hand or has a draw to a hand that will be second-best to yours.

As an example, suppose you're in middle position with

You called the blinds, got another caller behind you, and were raised by a player in late position. Everyone who entered the pot for one bet calls the raise. Assume the flop is

giving you the nut flush. The fact that an ace appeared on the flop not only made you the nut flush, it probably gave one or more of your opponents a pair of aces or possibly two pair.

Aggressive players will often bet their pair of aces into a three-suited board to see where they stand. Their objective is to drive out anyone holding a mid-range diamond who might outdraw them if they could see free cards on the turn or river to catch a fourth diamond.

If the player with aces is raised, it will usually come from someone holding either two pair or a small- to mid-sized flush. If one of your opponents held 6♦ 7♦ and was bet into by someone holding a pair of aces, he should raise to make it expensive for anyone holding a large, singleton diamond to outdraw him. When the flop is three-suited, most of the betting and raising on the flop is not aimed at getting more money into the pot. It is designed to make it too costly for drawing hands to stick around and get lucky.

If you hold the *nut flush* your interest lies not in reducing the number of opponents but in luring them onward — to the turn and the river, when bets double and you can extract maximum profit from them. Your strategy in this case is simple. Most of the time you're going to quietly call and hope to keep others in the pot with you.

With monster hands you're hoping someone else makes a good hand, then you can raise or reraise when betting limits double. If you're in a $1–$4–$8–$8 game, you don't want to reveal the strength of your hand by raising, check-raising, or reraising until the turn. If you think your opponent might fold if you raise on the turn, just call — then raise on the river.

Knowing your opponents is important. Some always call when they've been raised on the turn, unless they're bluffing with a trash hand. Others will throw away a *good* hand if they figure a raise means you've got a *better* one. With the first opponent you're much better off raising the turn and betting out after he's checked to you on the river. With the latter, you might just call his bet on the turn. He'll think he has the best hand and you'll probably elicit another bet from him on the river. If so, you can raise. Many opponents — who might otherwise have thrown their hand away if they were raised on the turn — will call that last raise on the river.

Terrific Flops

Flopping a set or top two pair with a safe board is one you'll like. To repeat, be sure the board is safe before you *slow-play* these hands. If, for example, you hold A–Q and the flop contains A–Q–4 of mixed suits, there's little chance that you're beaten or even up against a good draw. While you usually want to avoid giving an opponent a free card, with this flop there are not too many cards that can hurt you. Since the board contains mixed suits there is no flush draw, and any straight draw is to an inside straight. Sure, you could be up against an opponent holding a 5–4, and if another four comes on the turn, he will have taken the lead with trips. But that opponent only has two cards in the deck that can help him — and if he's willing to stick around in the face of such odds, you'll earn so much from him in the long run that losing an occasional hand to an 11-to-1 longshot shouldn't bother you.

Flopping Three-of-a-Kind

Anytime you flop a set, you're naturally going to assume you have the best hand. You'll be right most of the time. Suppose the pot was raised and reraised before the flop. You hold 9–9; the flop is A–Q–9. You have to consider the possibility that one of your opponents has a larger set. If he does, he probably won't do any raising on the flop. Like you, he'll be waiting in the weeds until the bets double on the turn.

In limit hold'em, you'll rarely release a set, especially when there is no probable flush or straight draws. But if you think you could be up against a bigger set, you might want to hold your fire when the raising starts on the turn.

You can really get hurt when it's set over set. Here's an example. You hold 7–7. The flop is 9–7–3. You will assume your set is the best hand. If one of your opponents holds 9–9, you will not realize that he also holds a set until you are reraised on the turn. When you lose a set-over-set hand, it will cost you some chips. Unfortunately, there's no way to avoid it. Here's the good news: This *bad beat* does not occur very often.

Flopping trips and losing with them is more common than set over set. Suppose you hold 8–7 and the flop comes 9–8–8. Now you're vulnerable in two ways. First, it's possible one of your opponents holds a hand like 9–8. If that's the case, he has flopped a full house and you're nearly drawing dead. Another possibility is that one of your opponents called an unraised pot with A–8 suited. Now you're outkicked, and your only out is to catch a seven or a *running pair* on the turn or river. You're also vulnerable to an opponent who may hold 7–6 for an open-end straight draw.

When two of your three-of-a-kind are paired on the board, it is not nearly as strong as holding the pair in your hand. The pair on board creates windows of vulnerability. While you probably have the best hand (and you will most of the time), the possibility that an opponent holds the same three-of-a-kind with a bigger kicker, or even a full house, must be factors to consider.

Good Flops

Two pair, an overpair, or top pair with a good kicker are another group of likeable flops. You need to be a bit more aware of your opponents' actions with these hands, however, since they are not unbeatable.

With two pair you can either bet out, or if the board looks safe enough, you can try for a check-raise if you believe one of your opponents will bet. When you hold top pair or an overpair, you should come out betting in the majority of cases. But if you're sure a player to your right will bet, trying for a check-raise allows you to narrow the field and increases your chances for winning. This is another one of those circumstances, like many in hold'em, where you have to consider the previous action, the size of the pot, and the proclivity of your opponents before making your decision.

When you are in late position, and your opponents have checked to you, you've got a decision to make. Are they checking poor hands and planning to fold if you bet, or are they checking very good hands, hoping for a bet so they can check-raise?

If you're in early position you might want to try for a check-raise; if successful, you'll be able to minimize your opposition and get additional money into a pot you're favored to win. But you're walking a fine line. You must avoid giving your opponents a free card, since that card might be the one they beat you with.

Dangerous Flops

Top pair with a marginal kicker, and second- or third-best pair are all dangerous flops. This does not mean they are unplayable, but you must strongly consider releasing your hand if you think you are beaten.

Top pair with a marginal kicker is always a troublesome hand. It's particularly troublesome if your top pair is aces, since many low-limit hold'em players routinely play any ace they're dealt — regardless of the kicker.

If you're holding A–9 and the flop is A–7–3 you have flopped top pair, but are you happy with it? If your opponent holds   A–J only three cards in the deck win the pot for you. You're drawing at a longshot, and unless that miracle nine turns, you're going to pay the price.

With second or third pair, your problem is determining whether any of your opponents hold a larger pair. Sometimes it's easy to tell. If, for example, there is a bet and a raise before it is your turn to act, your choice is simple. Throw your hand away.

Here's another example. Suppose you hold 8–7. The flop is 10–7–3 and your only opponent comes out betting. What should you do? Do you give him credit for a pair of 10s, or is he trying to steal the pot with a hand like Q–J? If your opponent holds a pair of 10s, or any overpair, you are a longshot. You need one of the two remaining sevens or one of the three remaining eights to win.

What's the key to making the right play? *Know your opponents!* Are they habitual bluffers or aggressive players who routinely try to steal when up against only one opponent? Are they rocks who never bet it unless they've got it? Most players are not found at either of those extremes, but somewhere in between.

When you're unsure, examine the quality of the flop for clues. Most of your opponents will play big cards far more frequently than small ones. If the flop contains two or more face cards and there's a bet, chances are someone holds a larger pair than yours. When the flop is ragged, there is less chance one of your opponents has paired the board. However, if you are in a hand with six-way action before the flop, it really makes no difference what the board looks like. When you're up against a lot of opponents, the flop will probably hit one of them. Again, we're back to fit or fold. If the flop doesn't provide sound reasons for continuing with your hand, toss it.

You'll occasionally flop what would ordinarily be a very good hand, but is dangerous because of the board's makeup. Assume you called with A–Q in middle position, two players to your left called, and the button raised. Only the blinds dropped out. Everyone else called the raise. Now the flop comes Q–J–J.

Do you like this hand? You've flopped two pair with the best possible kicker, but you're up against three opponents. One raised, and the others were strong enough to call him. This suggests they are playing *big* cards. Is one of these big cards a jack? Do any of your opponents hold big pairs — aces, kings or queens? This is not an easy decision to make. What could they have raised or called with? A–K or K–Q, or even smaller pairs, like 10s or nines, are possibilities. If they hold these hands you're in luck. But you're out of luck if one of your opponents called with a J–10, Q–J, K–J, A–J, J–J, Q–Q, K–K or A–A. Of course, with the last four hands they probably would have raised before the flop.

The best strategy might be to check, since betting will not drive out anyone holding a bigger hand than yours, and there are not many free cards that can beat you.

Another dangerous flop is top pair or top two pair, when the board is three-suited or sequenced. You might be up against a made straight or flush. Still, if you're going to play at all, you're better off betting to make it expensive for players holding a lone high card of that same suit, or a four-straight to draw out on you. There is no sure-fire way to tell whether anyone else has made a big hand. You'll get a clue by examining the board and knowing your opponents, but you'll seldom be positive. If you are uncertain, you might want to check and call to see where the strength comes from. This kind of situation takes a good deal of experience and judgment to play. If you're unsure of whether to continue under these circumstances, you probably ought to err on the side of caution.

Overcards

Should you play overcards or not? Many beginners and low-limit players routinely call with overcards. So do many players in bigger games. Assume you called the flop with K–J, you're up against three opponents, and the flop is 8–6–3 of mixed suits. What should you do if someone bets? Do you call, hoping the card you take off the deck is a king or a jack — one of the six remaining cards in the deck which presumably gives you the best hand? Or are you better off folding to wait for a flop that fits your hand?

The best clue in your decision-making process is to know your opponents. What kind of hands are they likely to play? Then examine the texture of the flop. Is it the kind of flop that tends to hit one or more players? Or is it so ragged that it's unlikely any of your opponents are holding cards the flop would have paired?

Be aware of how many opponents you're up against. Remember, the more opponents, the more likely the flop will hit at least one of them. If you're up against one opponent, you'll seldom be sure whether he's running a bluff or if the flop paired him. The decision to play or pass needs to be made with an understanding of your opponent's playing style, an awareness of the amount of money currently in the pot, and how much you're likely to win if you hit your hand. You should also consider your opponent's propensity for bluffing as well as the texture of the flop.

Finally, if you're unsure of what to do, my advice again is to err on the side of caution until you gain enough playing experience to feel comfortable under similar playing conditions.

Flopping a Draw

When you play sequenced or suited cards and flop a four-flush or a four-straight, you'll have to decide whether to continue with your draw. How do you make that decision?

It's not as automatic as it appears. First, you need enough opponents to make the anticipated pot odds offset the mathematical odds against hitting your hand. You also need to be certain that if you make your draw, it will be the winning hand.

How many opponents are enough? If you're up against three or more, you will get pot odds making it worthwhile to draw. When you're holding two large cards, such as A–Q, you're probably favored against any lone opponent regardless of whether you make your hand. You might, in addition to making your draw, pair either of your cards. Sometimes just your two big cards will be sufficient to win in a showdown.

Occasionally you'll flop a four-flush against a paired board. For example, you hold

and the flop is

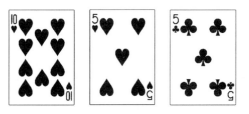

How does this affect your chances? Because the board is paired, it is possible that one of your opponents holds a set (which can improve to a full house). Maybe that opponent already made a full house or quads — in which case you're drawing dead. Does this mean you should throw your hand away?

No! This is not an automatic fold. Nevertheless, the added chances of being beaten by a full house or quads (impossible without a paired board) means the pot needs to offer a bigger potential payoff to offset the possibility of completing your hand and losing. If the implied odds — plus the money already in the pot — are sufficient to offset those few times you'll make your flush but lose to quads or a full house, go for it.

While flopping a four-flush into a paired board is a fairly common occurrence, making a flush and drawing dead to a full house or quads does not happen that frequently. Sometimes, however, you'll flop a four-flush, only to have your flush card on the turn or river pair the board. If there's been a lot of prior raising, one of your opponents may have been holding a set. Now he has a full house, and you're beaten. When that happens, there's not much you can do but be aware of the possibilities and save a bet on the turn or river. You've simply been outdrawn — and it's frustrating.

Multiway Possibilities

You'll occasionally flop hands that offer more than one possibility. Assume you hold 8♥ 7♥ and the flop is 7-6-5 and the five is a heart. You've flopped top pair, a straight draw, and a potential *backdoor flush*.

When you flop a hand with more than one way to win, your hand is stronger than any of its individual components. In this case, your top pair might win by itself, could improve to trips or two pair, make a straight on the turn or river, or make a flush if hearts fall on the turn and river.

Here's another example. You hold

and the flop is

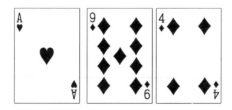

Unless there was a lot of action prior to the flop, chances are you now hold the best hand, and are favored to win even if your hand does not improve. You also have opportunities for improvement.

With a hand this promising you want action. Get more money into the pot by betting or raising. Check-raise if you think one of your opponents will bet into you. You might hold the best hand right now. Even if you don't, nine cards (the remaining diamonds) give you the nut flush. If any of the remaining three jacks fall, you'll have two pair. Another ace gives you trips, and reduces the chances that one of your opponents also holds an ace.

Your real concern is not that any of your opponents hold an ace, but whether he holds it with a king, queen, nine, or four kicker. The worst scenario, of course, is that your opponent holds A–A. You beat all but A–A, A–K, A–Q, A–9, or A–4. Your opponent's A–J will split the pot, while any of the other seven possible A–x holdings win it for you.

Summary

- Regardless of how promising your starting cards may have looked, if the flop doesn't fit your hand, most of the time you'll have to release it. But if you have big cards against few opponents, you might bet. Still, the general rule is this: *The flop defines your hand.*

- If you're not certain about your opponents' actions on the flop, assess the flop against their actions. Be aware of their playing style. Determine if they're passive or aggressive, loose or tight. Categorize their play.

- When you're up against a lot of opponents, fold if the flop does not fit your hand. It probably fit somebody's hand — regardless of how ragged it might look. Let some other fool call to keep the bettor honest. Save your money for profit-making opportunities.

- When you flop a big hand, give your opponents an opportunity to make the second-best hand, but avoid giving them a free card that could beat you.

- If you flop a draw, stick with it as long as the pot odds promise a greater payoff than the odds against making your hand. When you have a hand with multiway possibilities, play it fast. It has value which exceeds any of its component possibilities.

- Be selective about the hands you plan to continue with, but be aggressive when you have a hand that warrants it.

Chapter 9

Quite a few poker theorists have suggested that the turn plays itself. That theory may be a holdover from seven-card stud, where conventional wisdom dictates that when you see fifth street, most of the time you've bought a through ticket to the river.

That's not quite the case in hold'em. There are decisions you'll have to make, and you can't play the turn on autopilot. But you shouldn't get yourself into too much trouble unless you've already made the mistake of seeing the turn when you shouldn't have. If that's the case, you're chasing and probably throwing good money after bad.

Most of the time you won't even see the turn. You'll have thrown away the majority of your hands before the flop, and mucked others once you saw the flop did not fit them. You need a valid reason for seeing the turn.

If there's no logical reason to be in the pot by the turn, you should have folded. It's very easy to squander your bankroll one bet at a time. Many low-limit players do just that, calling one more bet and then another. While calling any one bet might be insignificant by itself, collectively it can break you.

If you've made it to the turn, you should be holding a good hand, a promising draw, or believe your bluff (or semibluff) can pick up the pot.

What to Do When You Improve

Your hand can improve on the turn in one of two ways. The first, and best, is when the turn card completes your flush or straight. You can also improve when the turn card converts your holdings into three-of-a-kind, two pair, or an overpair. You've also benefited if you had a good hand going in, and the turn — while not improving your hand — did not improve your opponents' either.

For example, suppose you hold Q–J and flop Q–J–6 of mixed suits. Chances are you have the best hand. Even if the turn card does not improve your hand, you're still likely to hold the best hand. While any turn card could conceivably make a set for an opponent holding a pocket pair of that same rank or an ace, king, 10, nine, or eight could make a straight, chances are against it.

When you have top two pair on the turn and an opponent bets, you should usually raise. If you're in early position, check with the intention of raising if you are fairly certain that one of your opponents will bet. If you think your opponents will check, go ahead and bet. If you are in late position and none of your opponents have acted, you should bet.

If you have the best hand, betting gets the maximum amount of money in the pot and makes it expensive for anyone to draw out on you. But it's not a totally risk-free strategy. If your opponent has has a set or turned a straight, you can count on being raised or reraised.

If you raise and are reraised, your opponent probably made a set or a straight. But if you bet and are raised, your opponent could also have two pair — and since you're playing the top two pair, his will be smaller.

Assume the turn card is a seven. Everyone checks, you bet, and are raised by the big blind. Since the big blind had a free play, he could be holding anything. He might have J–7 or Q–7, and is now raising because he thinks his two pair is the best hand. You won't be sure what he's holding, but knowing his playing style will frequently provide clues.

If you're playing in a jackpot game and the turn gives you a hand that would qualify for the jackpot (aces full or better in most jackpot games), ask yourself if there's an opportunity for a jackpot. If there is a pair on board, or the possibility of a straight flush, you certainly don't want to play so aggressively that you'll drive out an opponent who might catch a miracle card on the river.

If you get really lucky, your opponent will make four-of-a-kind or a straight flush — and you'll walk away with the lion's share of the jackpot. On the other hand, hitting the jackpot is a real longshot. Since chances of hitting it are small, you still want to get as much money into the pot as you can. You're an overwhelming favorite and, to repeat, *you want to get as much money in the pot as you can* when you're holding a real monster hand.

When You Don't Improve

Most of the time the turn card will not help you. It's unfortunate, but true. So what should you do? The answer depends on the kind of hand you have, as well as the relationship between the pot odds and your chances of making your hand on the river.

If you have an open-ended straight or flush draw, and you're up against two or more opponents, usually call any bet on the turn. However, if the board is paired, and there's a bet and raise in front of you, be wary. You might be up against a full house. If you are, you're drawing dead.

You could also be up against a set or two pair. The strongest clues to which hands you're facing lie in knowing your opponents. If one of your opponents is someone who never raises a three-suited board unless he can beat a probable flush, release your hand.

Your basic strategy on how to play the turn should include:

- Betting or checking with the intention of raising when you're sure you have the best hand.

- Making it expensive for opponents who hold lesser hands, or who are on the come, to draw out on you.

- Usually trying to get to the river as cheaply as possible when you're on a draw.

- Betting — rather than checking and calling — if you think it will cause your opponent to fold.

- Being alert to picking up a draw on the turn. It may allow you to continue playing a hand you otherwise should throw away.

Occasionally you'll find yourself in a pot with lots of callers for the flop. Let's say you hold 9–8 on the button and you flop 10–8–6. You don't have top pair, your kicker is weak, and your draw is to an inside straight. Even so, with enough players calling the flop, you're getting sufficient odds to take a card off the deck.

Now suppose the turn card is a king. Suddenly there's a bet up front. Most of the remaining players fold. Now there are not enough callers to offer the proper odds. In addition, the cost of bets usually doubles on the turn, so unless there's already sufficient money in the pot to justify continuing, wait till next hand.

If you're in a $3–$6 game the cost has escalated to $6, or $12 if you're raised. If you don't improve, you're probably beaten. Even if you hit your hand, there's one less round to extract extra bets from your opponents.

If you made your straight on the turn, and someone bets in front of you, your raise would trap your opponents for an additional bet, plus whatever you could gain on the last round of betting.

If you're playing in a $1–$4–$8–$8 spread-limit game, the cost on the last two betting rounds more than doubles. In a game with this betting structure, there is often good reason to continue with a longshot, in order to see if the turn card makes your hand. If the turn doesn't help and there is a bet in front of you, not only has the cost of betting gone up, but the number of future betting rounds has decreased. You have less opportunity to punish your opponents if you make your hand.

Should I Continue With My Draw?

Flopping a four-flush or an open-ended straight is a common occurence. If it's relatively inexpensive, you'll invariably stay for the turn card — particularly when you're certain yours will be the best hand if you make it. But most of the time the turn card will be a stiff. After all, if you've flopped a four-flush there are only nine other cards of your suit remaining in the deck or in someone's hand.

If you've flopped an open-ended straight draw, only eight of 47 cards will help you. With two cards to come, you have a 35 percent chance of making your flush, and a 31.5 percent chance of making a straight. Expressed in odds, that's 1.86-to-1, and 2.17-to-1 against making a flush or straight. Most of the time, you're going to have to decide whether to take another card off the deck. How should you determine your move?

While many low-limit players stay with any draw all the way to the river, regardless of pot size or the number of opponents, there's a better way to go about it. Here's what to do. Estimate the current size of the pot as well as how many opponents will stick around and pay you off if you get lucky.

If the estimated payoff is 2.5-to-1 or better, then either draw will show a positive expectation in the long run. What does this mean? If you could replay a similar hand thousands of times, you'd show a profit by making this play. If the estimated payoff was only even money, however, you'd show a loss in the long run.

Deciding whether to continue with a draw seems to baffle many beginners. It shouldn't. It is simply another instance of mentally calculating how much the payoff will be if you win, and comparing that figure to the odds against making your hand. If it's favorable, go for it. If it's not, don't.

The process of estimating pot odds versus the odds against hitting your hand can be confounded by the possibility that you'll occasionally hit your hand but lose.

Suppose you're holding

and the flop is

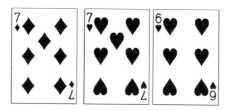

You've got a draw to the nut flush. But you may be up against a full house or trips that can improve to a full house. The presence of a pair on board should be a warning to any flush or straight draws.

Some authors have suggested that continuing with a draw under these circumstances is suicidal. I don't agree. I believe you can continue, but you need somewhat higher pot odds to offset those instances when you make your hand and lose with it.

Losing with the nut flush doesn't happen all that often. When it does, you'll know it. You'll bet or raise, only to be raised or reraised. Is it a bluff? Does your opponent have a full house or did he make the mistake of raising with a smaller flush than yours?

You have to know your opponents. It's no fun to throw away the nut flush in the face of an apparent full house, but against the kind of player who never makes a move unless he's got the goods, I'll toss my flush most of the time. In fact, in most lower-limit games, when you're reraised on the turn, your opponent will have a hand. Unless you're up against an absolute maniac, you'd better give him credit for a hand, and a big one at that.

Sometimes you'll make your flush, only to be up against another one. Your concern, of course, is whether yours is bigger. If you hold the nut flush, there's no problem. Your only dilemma is how to extract the maximum possible profit from your opponent. If you called the flop with a hand like 10–9 suited, and make a flush on the turn, what should you do if there's a bet and raise in front of you? Sure, the bettor might have top pair, two pair, or a set — all of which you can beat — but what does the raiser have? He could have a smaller flush than yours — or a bigger one. What's the best play?

In most cases, you shouldn't raise or reraise unless you're sure you'll have the best hand if you're called. Many seemingly adept players figure they can raise anytime they think they've got the best hand, never considering the possibilities that they could be reraised. Because there is always the possibility that you'll be beaten by an opponent who calls your raise, as well as the possibility that you might also be reraised, raise only when you have a hand that figures to win if it is called.

One of poker's most frustrating moments occurs whenever you turn a straight or a flush and are beaten. When it happens, it will try your patience. If you feel a sense of frustration, or a strong case of "Why me? Dear God, why me?" then it is time to get up from the table and walk around until you cool down. When big hands get beaten, lots of otherwise good players go on tilt and will start to throw off a lot more money than that hand cost them. If it's any consolation, take solace in the fact that your big hands will hold up most of the time.

Should I Check-raise or Should I Lead?

This question comes up frequently. You're in early position. You hold Q–J and flop an open-ended straight draw when 10–9–5 show up on board. An eight appears on the turn and you make a straight. It's also possible one of your opponents holding 7–6 or J–7 makes a smaller straight. You would love to see this, since they can't im- prove.

If you try for a check-raise and your opponents all check behind you, you've cost yourself more money.

So what's the best course of action? Should you bet, hoping to get some more money into the pot? Or are you better off check-raising and trying for a bigger payday, bearing in mind that you might not get *any* money into the pot if they all check behind you?

Do some detective work. Put on your Sherlock Holmes hat or Lieutenant Colombo raincoat. Reconstruct the play of the hand. Was there a lot of preflop action, suggesting that your opponents held big hands or big pairs? Did they raise on the flop, suggesting they might have been trying to force any straight draws to fold? Or did they just check and call, suggesting that they, too, were on the come and have now made their hands?

An opponent holding a single big pair might also check, since the turn showed straight possibilities. He could also bet to see where he's at, and fold if raised. If you think this is the case, you're better off leading with a bet. He may call, but would throw his hand away if he bet first and you raised him.

If your opponent was also on a draw, you might want to check, hoping he will try to steal it with a bluff. Another possibility is that he made his straight, and though smaller than yours, he'll still bet from late position. If that's the case, you can raise, with the assur- ance he will not lay his hand down even if he suspects you have the nut straight.

This is a case where recalling the play of the hand is more impor- tant than knowing the tendencies of your opponents. If you can de- duce what kind of hand — or hands — your opponents are likely to hold, you can decide whether to come out betting or try for a check-raise. Remember, unless you think your opponent will bet and call your raise, betting is the preferred course of action.

That's especially true if your opponents are very aggressive. If you bet, you may be fortunate enough to have your opponent raise, and with the nut straight, you'll be able to make it three bets.

Bluffing On the Turn
Suppose you raised with A–K before the flop, then bet into two op- ponents when the flop came J–7–3. You don't suspect any strength;

you know your opponents are solid enough players to release a hand when they think they're beaten.

Because your opponents have to consider the possibility that you're holding an overpair or a jack with a good kicker, it will be difficult for them to call with anything less than a J–8. Of course, if your opponents are calling stations, they'll call you with J–x, 7–x, and probably 3–x. You're going to find a smattering of calling stations in lower-limit games, and you'll have to become adept enough at knowing your opponents proclivities, so you don't try to bluff players who never release a hand.

A good player understands that you might be betting a hand like A–K. He may not call even if he holds a hand like 8–7, since he can't be certain about what you have and could be beaten if his inclination about your bluff is wrong. Of course, when a good opponent strongly suspects you're trying to steal the pot with Big Slick, you can expect him to raise with 8–7, since he knows you'll throw away two overcards in the face of a raise, rather than call an additional bet on the small chance that an ace or king will fall on the turn or river. Although a *semibluff raise* is not a common play, it is a very strong one when used sparingly.

Your bet may cause your opponent to lay down the best hand. If he calls, the turn or river could bring an ace or king and win the pot for you. But if you bet and are raised, throw your hand away. Sure, someone might be making a move on you. But it doesn't happen frequently enough to worry about, particularly in low-limit games. Most of the time you'll be beaten when you're raised.

Here are some hints to help you decide whether to bluff on the turn:

- Don't bluff bad players. They're brain dead to the clues you're broadcasting. To beat a bad player, you're simply going to have to show down the best hand. You'll beat bad players because you'll lose less with your bad hands than they will, and you'll extract more money from them with your good hands.

- Mentally review the way the hand has been played. Would your betting/raising pattern cause a good player to assume you're holding a big hand? If your opponent doesn't believe you're holding a bigger hand than his, don't waste your time trying to bluff.

- Know your opponents. Will they release a hand, or are they calling stations who believe they must call to keep you honest?

- How much money is in the pot? The larger the pot, the more likely someone will call simply for the size of the pot. Most players will abandon a small pot more readily than a big one.

- Do you think your opponent is on the come, and will release his hand if he does not improve on the turn?

Summary

Quite a few theorists have offered the opinion that the turn plays itself. That's not quite the case in hold'em. There are important decisions to make on the turn.

- When you've got the top two pair on the turn and an opponent bets, you should raise, unless a strong possibility of a straight or flush exists.

- If you're playing in a jackpot game and the turn gives you a hand that would qualify for the jackpot, don't play so aggressively that you drive out an opponent who might catch a miracle card on the river.

- If you've got an open-ended straight draw or a flush draw, and you're up against two or more opponents, call any bet on the turn. However, if the board pairs, and there's a bet and raise in front of you, be wary. You could be up against a full house.

- Bet, or check (planning to raise) when you're sure you have the best hand. Make it expensive for opponents who are on the come to draw out on you.

- If you hold drawing cards, usually try to make your hand as cheaply as possible.

- If you have a hand you would call with, betting — rather than calling — is a superior strategy if you think there's any chance your bet will cause your opponent to fold.

- Be alert to picking up a draw on the turn. It may allow you to continue playing a hand you otherwise would throw away.

- "Should I check-raise or should I bet?" comes up frequently. Unless you think your opponent will bet and call your raise, you should come out betting.

- Don't bluff bad players.

Chapter 10

*I*f you're still contesting the pot while awaiting the river card, you should have a strong hand or a draw to what you believe will be the best hand if you make it. If you're playing with reasonably prudent opponents, what may have begun as a confrontation between many opponents before the flop probably will be reduced to two — or perhaps three — once all the board cards have been exposed.

Realized Versus Potential Value

Because there are no more cards to come once the river card has been dealt, your strategy must be very different at this point. Prior to the flop, as well as on the flop and turn, many strategic considerations are predicated on your chances of subsequent improvement. You could, for example, bet a hand comprised of a pair and a four-flush. Not only might your pair be the best hand at the point, your bet could force a better hand to fold — not to mention the flush you could make if a third suited card appears on the turn or the river.

Your hand has equity, or value, from many sources. Taken together, your pair, with its potential for a flush or the possibility of improvement to two pair or trips, make it a valuable hand. And its worth is made up of realized value plus potential value.

Once the river card is exposed, your hand no longer has any *potential* value. Its value has been fully realized — for better or worse. If the flush draw never materializes, you're left with one pair, and it may not be enough to win the pot. More importantly, your strategic thinking has to change too.

Apart from a naked bluff, your decision to check or bet if no one has acted, or fold, call, raise, or reraise if there has been action, can only be based on the realized value of your hand.

What Should I Do if I Make My Draw?

Many beginners and low-limit players will automatically check a good flush from early position hoping to trap their opponents for an additional bet. Others automatically bet whenever they make a flush. These are two very different strategies. Which, you may wonder, is correct?

Before you read on, think about the last four or five drawing hands you made. How did you play them? Did you bet your straight or flush or did you try for a check-raise? What was your decision based on? Did you act out of habit? Was it a gut reaction to the texture of the game? Something guided your actions. Do you recall what it was?

Here's part one of the general rule on check-raising. Do it when you believe you will have the best hand most of the time you *are called*. Remember, believing you have the best hand is not enough to justify a check-raise. Sometimes your hand will not be the best one, and you'll find yourself facing a reraise. To compensate for these occasions, only check-raise when you believe you will hold the winning hand if you are called — unless, of course, you believe check-raising will cause your opponent to lay down a better hand.

Part two of the general rule on check-raising states that you need to be fairly certain your opponent will bet if you check. It's no fun to check a big hand only to have your opponents check behind you, especially when you know they would have called — if only you had bet.

If you are not certain you'll hold the best hand if called, or you aren't sure one of your opponents will bet if you check, do not check-raise. Unless you can answer "yes" to both of these questions, bet. Don't check-raise.

Sometimes even aggressive opponents who have been betting the entire way will slow down when a third suited card appears on board. Since they've been doing the betting and you've been calling, it's natural for them to assume you're on the come. When that third suited card appears or an apparent straight is on board, many players — even aggressive ones — apply the brakes.

If you're going to check-raise when it appears you're trying for a flush, you need to be certain that your opponent is aggressive enough to bet right into that flush or straight draw. It helps if you can delude your opponents into thinking you do not have a come hand. Here's how. Suppose you're in early position with

You're raised. You call. The flop comes:

Now suppose you bet. If your opponent holds A–A, K–K, Q–Q, or A–Q, you'll probably be raised. When you check and call if a blank falls on the turn, your opponent may now assume you were either trying to steal the pot from early position, "testing" your kicker with a hand like Q–9 or Q–8, or were betting second pair to find out where you stood.

He may no longer put you on a flush draw. If you make your flush on the river, you've set your opponent up for a check-raise. Believing you were checking a lesser hand on the turn or river, your opponent, especially if he is aggressive, will come out betting. Now he's trapped. When you raise, he'll realize you've probably got him beat, but not many beginners or low-limit players will throw their hand away for one additional bet. They'll make a crying call, but they'll pay you off.

Here's another advantage. By betting a four-flush on the flop and checking the turn, you've enabled yourself to bet other marginal hands on the flop to get a free card on the turn when there's a threatening board. Because you baited the check-raising trap so successfully, you've created some deception in your game. Deception allows you to extract additional money from your opponents, or see the turn for free, since they will not be certain about your hand.

This, of course, only works against opponents who are astute enough to put you on a hand, and then see whether your holdings confirm their supposition. When they're wrong, you will have created some additional maneuvering room for yourself since those opponents will no longer be able to trust their judgment. Of course, when your opponents are absolute maniacs, compulsive callers, or just brain dead, don't waste any energy trying to fake them out. They will do what their whims and proclivities tell them, regardless of any seeds of misinformation you might have scattered in their direction.

With a maniac, you don't need to set up a check-raise. He's going to bet most of the time, and you can snap him off whenever you're holding a better hand. With a calling station, don't check-raise. Just keep betting if you've got the best of it. You'll have to show the best hand to win, but you'll always get paid off.

Making Two Pair On the River

Suppose you're in the big blind with A–7. The pot isn't raised, and you flop A–J–4 of mixed suits. You call a bet on the flop and again on the turn. Now the board looks like this: A–J–4–2. You're up against two opponents. At least one, and possibly both of them have an ace. While you don't figure either of them for A–K, A–Q, A–J, since they probably would have raised with such hands, you might put them on A–10, A–9 or A–8. An ace with a kicker worse than yours is also a possibility. You're not sure whether you're beaten, but you keep calling. If a seven comes on the river, go ahead and bet.

If your opponent is holding a hand like A–10, he won't be sure whether his is the best hand, and will probably show it down if you check. If you bet, your opponent will probably call. If someone bets and you're in later position and certain you're not up against a set or A–J, go ahead and raise. If your opponent had flopped a set or top two pair, he probably would have checked the flop, trying for a check-raise on the turn. Instead, he bet all the way. Since he didn't try for a check-raise, it's unlikely he has a powerhouse, and your two pair is likely to be the best hand.

If your opponent turned a set, he would have bet the turn since you checked into him. Since he would also bet top pair you won't know with absolute certainty what he's holding. If he's turned a set, he will raise, and with two pair, you'll have to pay him off. But turning a set occurs infrequently, and it's a risk you can afford to take.

If you're holding two pair, and the turn or river brings a third suited card, be careful. If one of your opponents was also calling along with you, he could have made a flush. While it is tough to throw away two pair, sometimes you have to. Some opponents are so tight they never bluff in these situations. If that's the guy who's betting when the flush card hits the board, you're better off souping your hand.

Boards that portend straights are more difficult to assess than flush boards. While any three suited cards are equally likely to produce a flush, and boards like J–9–8–7–5 and Q–10–6–3–2 can both produce straights, the former is much more likely to yield one than the latter. So much so, that if you held J–9 against multiple opponents you'd almost never bet into that first board. But if you held Q–10 against the latter board, you'd be itching for an opportunity to raise.

Top Pair On the River

An enduring dilemma is what to do on the river when you're holding top pair against one or two opponents. All the cards are out. Now you have to decide whether to check or bet, or, if your opponent acts first, whether to call, fold, or raise.

If you're observant, you will notice that some opponents will usually bet top pair on the river, unless there is a strong threat of a flush or straight. Others seldom bet one pair for value even when the board is not threatening. Most, however, fall somewhere in between; they treat this situation as a judgment call. There is no magic formula to determine the best course of action, but there are some things you can do to clarify your decision.

Suppose you hold A–K. You raised before the flop and have two callers. You bet the flop and the turn. Now the board shows A–Q–4–7–9 of mixed suits. All the cards are out and it's your turn to act. Do you bet or check? How should you evaluate your move?

You'll beat any pair, but lose to any two pair. Unless one of your callers held a pocket pair of nines and made a set on the river, you can probably dismiss the notion that there is a set out against you. If one of your opponents either flopped or turned a set, he would have raised on the turn when the betting limits doubled.

Your real concern, of course, is whether one of your opponents holds two pair. If an opponent held A–Q, he probably would have raised before the flop, called on the flop, and raised your bet on the turn. An opponent holding A–7, A–4, Q–4 or Q–7 would probably have raised on the turn. You have two concerns: How will your opponents play when they are not sure whether they hold the best hand, and if you bet, will your hand be the best one if it is called?

If your opponents are the type who would raise with any two pair and call with lesser hands, like A–8 or Q–J, you'll want to bet. If they had made two pair on the turn, that's when they would have raised. Unless they are holding A–9, Q–9, 9–7, A–4, A–7, Q–4, Q–7, 4–7, or 9–4, your bet on the river will elicit a call, and you'll win.

Now imagine the same scenario, but this time your opponent is *first* to act. If he bets, should you fold, call, or raise, and if he checks, should you bet?

If your opponent is very aggressive and tends to overplay weak hands, you can raise if you suspect he is betting a hand that is weaker than yours. If he is a tight player, just call his bet. If he is a real rock who seldom, if ever, bluffs, then throw away top pair with anything less than a very big kicker whenever he bets on the river. Since you are holding a king kicker, in this case you would call.

The key, of course, is knowing your opponents and their playing tendencies. Top pair on the river is a very common play, and it is critically important that you learn to play it well.

Another commonly encountered play occurs when you hold top pair with a marginal kicker. Suppose you called the flop in late position with

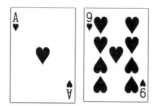

By the river, the board looks like this:

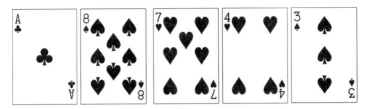

You flopped top pair with a back-door flush possibility. You called the flop along with a player behind you, and picked up the nut flush draw on the turn. The river card was a total blank. Your opponent — the one who has been betting all the way — bets again. What should you do?

Should you call automatically with top pair? Do you give the bettor credit for an ace, and assume he's got a bigger kicker? What about the player behind you? He, too, has been calling all the way. What could he have, you wonder — an ace with a bad kicker, a busted straight or flush draw, or perhaps two small pair? There's a reason he's been calling. If he had a big set or top two pair, you can be fairly certain he would have raised on the turn — trapping both the bettor and you for two bets.

But he didn't. He's been quietly calling. So he probably doesn't have a great hand, but he may have a good one.

Should you raise the bettor? A raise would probably prevent the last player from overcalling with a hand like A–10. If that's the case, you'll win if the original bettor was either bluffing or betting a hand like A–5 or 9–8.

Are you better off throwing it away, assuming that the bettor's kicker is superior to yours and your opponent in last position may have two small pair that he'd call with — but not bet? The answer lies again in knowing the playing tendencies of your opponents, as well as the size of the pot.

Big Pots On the River
Pots often grow quite large by the river, particularly when there has been a raise before the flop. This can cause a lot of players to marry the pot. If the flop brings a four-flush or straight draw to your opponents, you can be certain they'll be there to the river.

If the straight or flush cards fail to come, a bet will usually drop any opponents who were trailing along hoping to make a straight or flush. Often there are only two or three opponents contesting a very large pot on the river.

You might be holding second pair, or perhaps top pair with a marginal kicker, when your opponent comes out betting. You're holding a hand you'd throw away if the pot were small, but with all that money in it, what should you do?

Suppose you're playing in a $3–$6 hold'em game and the pot is $90 by the time you reach the river. If your opponent bets, the pot now contains $96. It is offering you 16-to-1 on your money. If you call and are beaten it will only cost you an additional $6.

If you throw your hand away and your opponent was bluffing, you made a $96 mistake.

The answer should be obvious. If you believe your opponent would bluff more than one time in 16, go ahead and call. Only if you are positive your opponent would never bluff, can you comfortably throw your hand away.

Generally you're better off committing the small error of calling with a losing hand, than the catastrophic error of folding a winner. In the hand cited above, even if your opponent would only bluff one time in 10, you are far better off calling than folding.

If you were to call 10 times, you'd lose $6 on nine occasions, for a loss of $54. On the tenth occasion, you'd win a $96 pot, for a net profit of $42. If you divide that $42 profit by each of the 10 times you called, your decision to call is worth $4.20 each time you make it — regardless of whether you win that particular pot.

If you are second to act, and think there's some chance you have the best hand, even if you don't consider yourself the favorite, you might want to raise if your opponent comes out betting. By doing this, you may get the third opponent to lay down his hand. If your first opponent was betting a fairly weak hand hoping you might fold, he, in turn, may now fold if he suspects you're holding a powerhouse. A play like this also adds some deception to your game. But like all deceptive plays, you have to use it sparingly.

Overcalling On the River

Occasionally you'll be last to act on the river against two or more opponents. If one bets and the other calls, what should you do?

With a bet and call in front of you, you'll have to credit at least one of your opponents with a legitimate hand.

While the first player might have been bluffing, the second player could not call unless he has a legitimate hand. While it is possible — although somewhat remote in lower-limit games that he could bluff-raise — there is just no reason to call unless you have a hand that figures to contend for the pot.

Consequently, you'll need a hand strong enough to beat a legitimate calling hand in order to overcall. If you would have raised had there been no caller, then you should definitely overcall. But if you have a hand which beats a bluff, but not much else, you'll save money by not overcalling.

Many players make a big mistake in low-limit games by overcalling when they know they're beaten. Consistently making crying overcalls can be costly. Unless you have a hand which is better than a calling hand, save your money for future opportunities.

Summary

Because all the cards on the board have been exposed by the river, your strategy must be very different at this point. Prior to the flop, as well as on the flop and turn, many strategic considerations are predicated on your chances of subsequent improvement.

- When the river card is exposed, your hand no longer has any potential value. Its value has been *realized*.

- Your decision to check or bet if no one has acted, or fold, call, raise, or reraise if there has been action, can only be based on your hand's realized value.

- Here's the general rule on check-raising: Do it if you believe you will have the best hand most of the time *you are called*.

- If you are not certain you'll have the best hand if you are called or you aren't sure one of your opponents will bet if you check, do not check-raise. Unless you can answer "yes" to both of these points, bet! Don't check-raise.

- When you make two pair it will usually be the best hand. But if the turn or river brings a third suited card, be careful, your opponent could have made a flush.

- When it's heads up and the pot is large, you're better off committing the small error of calling with the worst hand, than the catastrophic error of folding the winner.

- To overcall you need a hand strong enough to beat legitimate calling hands.

Part Three:

Post Graduate Work

... and pluck 'till time and times are done,
the silver apples of the moon,
the golden apples of the sun.

William Butler Yeats

Why Raise?

Raising is one of poker's eternal enigmas. Some players love to fire in raise after raise. The more action they create, the happier they are — never mind whether their cards justify it. Others never raise unless they're holding the nuts, and even then it's with trepidation.

Some players regularly raise from early position with a hand like A♠–8♠, believing that any suited ace is a powerhouse. Other players routinely raise in early position with hands like K–J or even Q–J. Some players always raise with Big Slick. Others, far fewer in number, treat A–K like any other drawing hand and just call with it.

Certain players raise from any position with a pair of sevens or bigger, regardless of the texture of the game. Others never raise with aces when they're in the blind because they fear giving away too much information about their hand.

Who's right? When should you raise? Why should you do it? To generate a plan of action, we need to explore the reasons to raise.

Here are five reasons to raise the pot in hold'em. Let's look at each of them individually.

Raising to Get More Money in the Pot

You've got a powerhouse hand. Someone bets, three players call, and it's your turn to act. What do you do? You raise, of course. You're holding a winner and want to build the pot, since it figures to migrate over to your stack of chips once the hand has been concluded.

Getting more money in the pot is the most common reason players raise. But you don't always have to hold the best hand to raise. Suppose you're on the button with:

and the flop is

It's a loose game. The blind comes out betting and four players call. Now it's your turn to act. You're getting 5-to-1 on your money, and with two cards to come the odds against making the nut flush are 1.86-to-1. Since this bet has a positive expectation, it is worth money each time you make it — regardless of whether you win this particular hand.

Since that's the case, go ahead and raise. You might as well earn as much as you can when you're lucky enough to hit your hand.

Raising to Eliminate Opponents

Suppose you've got a pair of queens. You're in fifth position and no one has called the blinds. Your pair of queens will play better against one or two opponents than a whole slew of them. Fire when ready. Go ahead and raise.

Here's another situation. You've got the same pair of queens, and you're in fifth position. The player to your immediate right raises. What should you do? Fire away. Make it three bets. If your opponent is the type who would raise with aces, kings, jacks or A–K, A–Q, A–J, K–Q, K–J or maybe even A–10 suited, chances are against him having a better hand than yours. Odds favor his holding two big cards. Go ahead and reraise. If the flop doesn't produce any overcards to your queens, you're the favorite.

If two overcards fall, you become an underdog, and ought to give it up if your opponent bets into you. If just one overcard falls and you're heads up, you're in the judgment zone, and unless you've got a terrific read on your opponent, you'll seldom be sure where you stand.

If he's clever, and tries for a check-raise by checking the flop and turn, go ahead and check behind him. If he bets the river, you're going to call, but you've also given him an opportunity to bluff with a hand that is worse than your pair of queens. But if you bet and he check-raises on the turn, you're probably beaten. Fold. But remember, when you've got a hand that plays better against fewer, rather than many opponents, raise or reraise to limit your opposition.

Raising to Get a Free Card on a More Expensive Street

You're last to act with a Q–J. The flop is 10–9–4 of mixed suits and you're facing three opponents. The player who is first to act bets, and is called by the others. Can you raise? Sure! If the turn card is not the king or eight you're looking for, the fact that you raised may enable you to see the river for free. And if you make the nut straight on the turn, your raise on the flop has gotten more money in a pot, which by all appearances will soon be yours.

Raising to Define Your Hand

I recall a game where I was last to act. I held kings, and I reraised a very strong player to my right. This is a player I consider one of the very best limit hold'em players in the Los Angeles area. Moreover, we are good friends, have discussed poker theory on many occasions, and each of us has a very solid understanding of the other's playing style.

The flop was:

My opponent bet, I raised, and he reraised. Because I know his play so well, I was sure he would not have bet if he flopped a set of aces. He would have checked the flop, called my bet and check-raised on the turn. I put him on A–K, with a smaller possibility he held a hand like A♥ J♥. The turn card was the 6♥. He bet, and I raised. He called. If he had flopped a set of aces, he would have reraised, since a set of aces was the best possible hand on the turn.

Now I was almost certain he held A–K. Since he knows my play very well, I was sure he would not have called with less than two pair. I was also quite sure my raise told him I had at least two pair, and more likely a set. When the 8♥ fell on the river he bet, I raised, and he reraised. It was then I knew my assessment was wrong. He could not possibly have A–K. He had to have entered the pot with a hand like A♥ J♥ and tried to steal the pot with his bet on the turn — since he had top pair with a reasonably good kicker, along with an opportunity to draw out if another heart fell on the river. That's exactly what happened. He made the nut flush. Although my analysis was correct, I was too late to save myself any money, and he won a big pot.

With the benefit of this instant replay, you can see how each of us, by virtue of our bets, raises and reraises, were defining our hands in terms of what we presumed the other was holding. Although I defined my set of kings against the possible hands he could have been holding, I incorrectly assumed he made two pair. While this was a costly error in judgment, you can learn something at my expense about raising and reraising to define your own hand against what you suspect your opponent might have.

Raising to Prevent a Free Card

Just as it is correct in certain situations to raise on the flop in order to gain a free card on the turn, it is also correct to raise in order to prevent your opponents from getting a free, or relatively inexpensive card.

Here's an example. You hold A–10 in fifth position. On the flop only three other players are active: the big blind, and seats eight and nine. The flop comes A–9–7. The big blind bets. With no raise before the flop, there's no way to determine what he might be holding. You may be outkicked if he holds A–K, A–Q, or A–J. If he holds A–9, A–7, or 9–7, you're also beaten. On the other hand, he may be betting with A–6, trying to win the pot right there if no one else holds an ace.

While you have some idea about the players in seats eight and nine, you're not certain you have the best hand. However, it's fair to assume that if either seats eight or nine had A–K, A–Q or A–J, they probably would have raised before the flop. While they may have called with a hand like A–5 suited, it's more likely they're holding connectors or a small pair. It is also possible one of them flopped a set, although the odds do not favor it. If they did, however, you'll not hear from them now. They'll wait and raise on the turn — when the bets double.

What should you do in this position? While calling is not a bad idea, raising is better. If the players in seats eight or nine hold hands like 10–9 or 9–8, they may call a single bet on the flop, hoping to catch a miracle card on the turn, or perhaps pick up a straight draw. However, if they are reasonably prudent players, they will not call a raised pot with second or third pair and little else to support it.

Is this a form of raising to thin out the field? Yes, it is. But in this case, you're doing so after the flop has defined — or partially defined — your opponents' hands. If it's the kind of flop that provides some help to your opponent, enough so he might stick around hoping to complete a draw if he can see another card for no more than a single bet, then a raise that forces him to fold is correct.

If your raise forces seats eight and nine to fold, you are heads up against the blind, and you have the added advantage of acting last on the turn and the river. You may also have the best hand. Unless the blind has flopped a big hand, like two pair or a set, he probably is not going to bet into you on the turn. This gives you the opportunity to check behind him. If he isn't holding much of a hand, and is an aggressive player, checking behind him may also elicit a bluff on the river, which you can easily snap off.

If he is not a particularly aggressive player, but tends to call too often with too little, you can bet the turn and the river without much fear of a raise, but with the certainty he will call you with marginal hands.

If, however, one of your opponents has flopped either a set or two pair, your strategy will fail. You'll be called on the flop, and when you bet the turn you'll be looking at a check-raise. If that's the case, you probably ought to fold, since it is hard to envision anyone raising with a hand worse than yours, unless they are fond of bluff-raising. Since you just don't see too many bluff-raises in lower limit games, you might as well assume you're beaten and save your money.

These five reasons to raise often act in concert with one another. While it is often correct to raise solely to limit the field, it is seldom worth a raise just to define your hand. By raising to limit the field, you will usually gain some information about how your hand stacks up against the competition.

If you raised with a pair of 10s and are reraised, there's bad news and good news in the air. You may well have achieved your goal of going heads up against one opponent, but you may also be beaten. If two overcards fall on the flop, assume you are beaten. The good news, scant as it may be, is that you've learned enough about the quality of your opponent's hand to save money by folding as soon as he bets the flop.

Summary

- Raising can be a dicey proposition. Most of the time you will not be entirely sure you have the best hand.

- By getting a fix on your opponents' play, you'll be able to tell which players are likely to be out of line when they raise.

- Don't let the fear of a reraise stop you from raising when proper strategy calls for it.

- Don't leave money on the table you could have won, but didn't, simply because you lacked absolute certainty about your opponent's hand.

- You are not playing to maximize your winning opportunities. If you did you'd simply play every hand, and you would go broke.

- You are not playing to minimize your losing opportunities. If you did, you'd play nothing but very big hands, and get no action when you did.

- Be aggressive enough to *optimize* your winnings. Optimize is the operative word!

Chapter 12

Analysis at the Table

*I*f you're a serious poker player, you know it's impossible to win consistently without exercising your mental muscles. The job of a poker player, like any job in the work-a-day world, is comprised of a variety of factors. Most of these factors in varying degrees are found in every job. Whether the job is as simple as sorting the big eggs from the small ones on a production line, or as complex as handling calculations in nuclear physics, each requires a specialized knowledge base. Each, although in varying degrees, requires critical thinking, problem solving, and accountability for results. In poker, you're free from the responsibilities of supervising others. Instead, you're an individual contributor. You, and you alone, are responsible for the results you achieve.

The job of a poker player is really one of gathering knowledge and being able to apply it during the heat of battle. Thinking on your feet is where the proverbial rubber meets the road, and it's important to examine the job of poker playing from this perspective.

I'm a Poker Player. How Much Thinking Does My Job Require?

Some jobs, such as police officers and firefighters, are characterized by a degree of danger and nasty environmental conditions. Certain professions require taking action and making decisions under a great deal of pressure. Others require a great deal of thinking. Research scientists, for example, spend much of their time thinking about very complex matters. And while they do make decisions, they are not usually made under severe time constraints. Perhaps the ultimate example in this category was Albert Einstein. Employed by the Institute for Advanced Studies at Princeton University, his job was merely to think about the nature of the universe and express it in mathematical terms!

Compare Einstein's profession to that of a commercial airline pilot. Although flying a big jet requires a great deal of technical skill, it is not a job requiring a lot of problem solving. Why? Because in emergencies, there is simply no time to leisurely engage in thought. When a warning light comes on and flames stream out of one of the engines as a pilot gazes out the cockpit window, he simply doesn't have the luxury of sitting back, crossing his legs, and saying to his co-pilot, "It looks like we're in some trouble. Now, let's chat a bit about how to handle that rather nasty looking fire out there."

No, that jet pilot has to react, and react immediately. In jobs where there's no time to think, successful practitioners draw the correct solution from simulated situations they've faced in training. That's why pilots spend a substantial amount of time in flight simulators and other training environments. When confronted with an emergency, they hope it's one they've encountered many times before in a controlled environment.

So what about poker? Is it a deep-thinking type of game like chess, or does it demand quick decision making? It's true that poker requires substantial thought. But it also requires quick decision making, since you do not have an unlimited amount of time at the table to decide whether to check, bet, or fold, call, raise, or reraise.

Poker Requires a Reservoir of Know-How

Poker requires quick reactions and adjustments. The successful player is able to quickly tap into a vast reservoir of information. Unlike chess, it is not a game that allows deep concentration and thought over an extended period of time. Success demands that you gain all the information and knowledge you can while you are away from the table. Like the jet pilot, once you are able to deal with difficult situations in a controlled or simulated environment, you'll be better able to make the correct decision in the real world. By putting your theoretical knowledge into practice you will mold it into practical know-how. Do this in low-limit games, however, before you attempt to ply your skills in big-money contests.

Decision Making at the Table

Although poker requires decisions to be made at the table, you can't subject each hand you encounter to lengthy analysis. You don't have the time or tools to take a play and run a 100,000-hand simulation on a computer to determine the best strategy. You have to act quickly.

Since you have only a short amount of time to make decisions, what kind of thinking and analysis should you be doing at the table?

Categorizing Your Opponents

The first rule of thinking or analysis at the table is to gather as much information as you can when you're not involved in a hand. Observe each of your opponents. Categorize their play: loose, tight, aggressive, weak-tight, calling station, prone to bluff, does most of his betting before the flop, likes to check-raise good hands on the turn, good player but currently on tilt, and so forth.

Since your playing strategy will be guided by the nature of your opponents, you need to categorize their play before you are faced with a decision when an opponent's playing style becomes a critical factor.

For example, suppose you raised before the flop with A–Q and by the turn the board shows Q–6–5–2 of mixed suits. You're up against one opponent who called your raise from the small blind. When you bet the turn, he raises. If you know your opponent is a very loose, habitually-bluffing, ram-and-jam player who is currently loosing and on tilt, you'd certainly call. You might even reraise. But if your opponent is a real rock who raises under identical conditions, you'd probably put him on an overpair, two pair, or a set, and throw your hand away.

None of this is very exotic from a strategic viewpoint. What's important is this: unless you invested the time in categorizing the play of your opponents *before* you were confronted with this particular hand, you'd have no other option than to guess about their play.

Not only is it important to categorize the play of your opponents, you have to keep doing this as long as you're in the game. Most of your opponents won't play the same way all the time. Many loose players play quite well for the first thirty minutes they're at the table. Then they get caught up in *gambling* and start to fly open.

At some point, they'll notice they're almost broke. Then they'll either tighten up dramatically or go to the other extreme. In a desperate attempt to recoup, they'll bet their last dollars on almost anything in a frenzied attempt to get even. If that miracle occurs and they do get even, watch out. That hitherto loose opponent will probably tighten up considerably — playing well in an attempt to hold on to the money he miraculously snatched from the lion's mouth.

During the play of a hand, you simply don't have time for complex analysis. If you have a substantial amount of game experience, you won't run into many game conditions that are entirely new. Most will be analogous to others you've faced before. That's why there is no substitute for real game experience, coupled with theoretical knowledge, and molded into practical know-how. Expertise at poker comes from an iterative cycle of reading and studying the game, playing the game, and thinking about the game. At some point, after seemingly endless cycles of repetition, you'll discover you're a much better player than most of your opponents.

Always be Aware of Pot Odds

No matter how much specialized knowledge you have stored in your poker toolbox, you're frequently forced to base your decisions on incomplete data.

In the heat of battle, regardless of whatever knowledge you might bring to the game, there is some decision making you've got to do. At a minimum you must always be aware of the pot size. While it is not critical that you mentally count each pot down to its last dollar, you do need to know approximately how much money is in the pot at any given time.

If you do not know how much the pot is offering you, there's no way to compare the odds against making your hand with the odds offered by the pot. You need to keep track of the pot in order to determine whether those pot odds warrant calling with hands where you need to improve in order to win.

Putting Your Opponents on Hands

It is also critical that you put your opponent on a hand. Many players make the mistake of putting their opponent on a single hand, but fail to change their assumption — even in the face of new information gained on subsequent betting rounds. A better way involves putting your opponent on groups of hands, then eliminating as many as you can by virtue of how he plays on succeeding streets.

Here's an example. You raise the blinds from fifth position with a pair of 10s. You're reraised by the player to your immediate left. The big blind calls for the two additional bets. You call too. Let's assume the raiser is an average player. He could have reraised with any one of a number of hands. Possibilities include any pair from jacks through aces. He could also have reraised on A–K, A–Q, A–

J, or even A–10 (though the latter three are not prime reraising hands) as well as with marginal hands like K–Q or K–J. If he raised with a big pair, he's in the lead. If he raised with big cards, you've got the edge.

Suppose the flop is 9–7–3 of mixed suits. The blind checks, you bet to test the quality of your hand. Your opponent raises. The big blind folds and you call. What kind of hand can you put him on now? For the most part, you can eliminate a set. He probably wouldn't have made it three bets before the flop with a pair of nines, sevens, or threes; and if he did, he'd just call the flop — planning to raise on the turn when the bets double.

He could have raised with any pair bigger than the highest board card. If he is a really aggressive player, he might bluff-raise with a hand like A–K, just in case he suspects you might be holding connectors like A–Q, A–J, or even A–K. Remember, at this point he isn't sure about your hand either, and he's trying to find out.

With a pair of 10s, you're not sure where you stand. If your opponent is playing big cards, you're in the lead. But if he does have a pair, it's undoubtedly bigger than yours. You call. The turn card comes, and it is an eight. Now you're holding top pair with a straight draw. You check and your opponent checks behind you.

Even though there are three sequenced cards on the board, you know your opponent is a good enough player to realize you probably would not have raised with a hand like J–10 and certainly would not have raised with 10–6 or 6–5. Consequently, you know he did not check because he thought you might have a straight.

You now presume he has a hand that cannot beat two pair, nor possibly one big pair.

At this point, you are putting him on big connectors, with a minute possibility that he might hold a pair of queens or jacks. Unless a jack or six falls on the river, you plan to check. If your opponent is playing big connectors, he might bet on the river, and you will gain one additional bet by snapping off his bluff. If he checks behind you, you have not cost yourself anything, since he probably would not have called your last bet without at least a big pair.

Even without playing this hand to its conclusion, you can see how you initially put your opponent on a fairly wide variety of possible hands, and through deductive reasoning based on observing the way the hand played out, it became possible to define your opponent's hand with some precision.

In real life, you have one other significant advantage. By knowing your opponents, you will have an even stronger line on their tendencies. Some players seldom bluff. Some will never bet out on the end with less than two pair, while others will always bet whenever they're holding top pair as long as the board is not threatening.

The better you know your opponents, the more secure you will be in making the correct decision under pressure. That's why you'll seldom see a top player bemoaning a hand he threw away. When a marginal player tosses a hand away, he'll inevitably spend time harping about the fact that he might have had the bettor beaten. The top player will be quite certain that his hand is not worth a call by the time he mucks it. Because of that, he is much less likely to make crying calls that have no chance of winning. As a result, he presents a much slimmer target for his opponents to shoot at — and saves money in the process. Remember, what you don't spend, you don't have to earn!

Summary

- You don't have unlimited time to think through complex confrontations and must be able to choose solutions from analogous hands you've encountered before.

- Think about various poker hands when you're away from the table.

- Supplement your thought processes by reading and studying poker theory.

- Continually categorize your opponents' play, since it will change and evolve over the course of the game.

- Be aware of the pot odds offered compared to the odds against making your hand.

- A decision to call — when you should have folded or betting when you should have checked — can cost you a bet or two. But a decision to fold when you should have called can cost you the entire pot.

Chapter 13

But They Were Suited

*E*ver since *Super System* was first published, there has been a continuing discourse threading its way through poker literature and cardroom conversations about the value and inherent worth of suited connectors. Back then I thought they were a lot more valuable than I do now. But that was because Doyle and the boys — fond as they were of playing hands like 8♣ 7♣ — were talking about no-limit hold'em, not the limit game most of us play.

They were onto something too. In a no-limit game, where the implied odds are theoretically infinite, and limited in practice only by the amount of chips your opponent has in front of him, one can play 8♣ 7♣ until the cows come home. Once they see the flop, skilled players will throw this holding away time after time, unless they make a big hand. Big hands in no-limit hold'em have a little bit extra going for them; they are deceptive. After all, when the flop helps a hand like 8-7, it's not quite as obvious as it is when an ace or king appears among the communal cards and your opponent comes out betting.

When you make a big hand with 8-7, your opponent is not likely to suspect it. This, of course, is when the expert pounces, causing his opponent to commit all his chips. Let's face it. You can afford to make a lot of one-bet calls with 8-7 in a no-limit game.

When you're playing no-limit poker — or pot limit, for that matter — one big hand can yield enormous returns. In limit hold'em, by comparison, an investment in a speculative holding such as 8-7 is not going to offer a return of the same magnitude. When the implied odds associated with any hand — never mind how big it may be — are constrained by the size of the wagers and number of raises permitted on each betting round, you can't break an opponent with one big, well-disguised hand.

Nevertheless, suited connectors can have a great deal of value in limit games too. But they can also get you into trouble, and it's worth thinking about how much inherent potential these hands have before committing chips to them.

I'm not talking about big suited connectors, like A♠ K♠ — everyone knows how valuable they are. And I'm not talking about trash hands like 3♥ 2♥. Even real gamblers can throw those puppies away.

But here I am, like the song says, "...stuck in the middle with you." I'm referring to hands like 10-9, 8-8, 8-7, and 7-6 — suited, of course. Since playing them correctly is so dependent upon the particulars of the hand one is involved in, some research, aimed at ferreting out the inherent strength of hands like these, was in order.

Before delving any more deeply into this, a cautionary word is in order. All the computer analyses conducted were *cold simulations.* And cold simulations are not real poker. In a cold simulation each hand plays on until the bitter end. In real poker games most players fold — at least some of the time.

The implications of this ought to be readily apparent. In real poker, stronger hands will win more often than they will in cold simulations. Weaker hands will not fares so well. How much better or worse depends on the nature of the hand. To get a sense of this, just ask yourself how much more readily you will fold 8♠ 7♠ than A♠ K♠, and how much more likely you are to fold A♠ K♠ than a pair of aces.

As you read through this chapter, it's important to bear in mind that cold simulations do not represent real poker. They are simply an attempt to generate some indication about the relative strength of mid-range suited connectors, and how they stack up against hands that are inherently more worthy.

Mike Caro's *Poker Probe* was used to run these cold simulations. For each of the seven different scenarios presented, one million hands of poker were simulated. That's probably three lifetimes of poker for the average professional poker player who's at the tables just about every day. Weekend players will have to outlive Methuselah to have any chance of playing as many real hands as one can easily simulate while eating dinner, answering E-mail, and doing laundry.

In the first simulation, 8♠ 7♠ was asked to play one million hands heads-up against A♠ K♠. Since all the flushes — with the exception of a few straight flushes that 8-7 is able to back into over the course of one million hands — belonged to Big Slick, the lower hand is dominated in suit, and can expect even fewer wins than it could in situations when its flushes would prove victorious.

Hand	Wins	Ties	Winning Percentage	Odds
All one suit				
A♠ K♠	632,277	5,508	63.5	.57:1
8♠ 7♠	362,215	5,508	36.5	1.74:1

In the "All one suit" scenario, A♠ K♠ won 632,277 of the million hands contested, while 8♠ 7♠ was victorious 362,215 times. The hands tied 5.508 times. A♠ K♠ won nearly two-thirds of the time, and was an odds-on favorite at.57:1. I was surprised to see that 8♠ 7♠ came out on top as frequently as it did, until I remembered that this confrontation was heads up, and each hand was played out until the very end. In a real poker game, how often do you think 8-7 would stick around if the flop did not provide any help, and there were a couple of overcards to contend with in addition to a wager from Big Slick?

In the second scenario, things got a bit better for 8-7. In this scenario, A♠ K♦ was matched against 8♠ 7♥. Rather than complete domination in suit, as was the case in the first analysis, this time only the spades belonged to A-K, while any four-card heart flushes would accrue to 8-7. Let's examine the results.

Hand	Wins	Ties	Winning Percentage	Odds
One suit dominated				
A♠ K♦	622,520	3,760	62.4	.6:1
8♠ 7♥	373,720	3,760	37.6	1.66:1

Since 8-7 would win whenever four communal hearts appeared on the board, it fared a bit better, though the results still weren't really worth writing home about. This time around, 8-7 was victorious in 373,720 hands, as compared to 362,215 when it was completely dominated in suit. Another ten thousand wins or so over the course of a million hands isn't much, and the percentages tell the story: A winning percentage of 37.6 compared to 36.5 is almost no difference at all.

In the third scenario, we took away the flush advantage enjoyed by A-K whenever it dominated 8-7 in suit. For this simulation, all the cards were of different suits, and A♣ K♥ was matched up against 8♦ 7♠. Before you look at the following chart, as yourself what you think the results should be. If you thought 8-7 would fare even better than it had in earlier analysis, you are correct. Improvement, however, was minute — an additional 6,000 hands won.

Hand	Wins	Ties	Winning Percentage	Odds
All cards of different suits				
A♣ K♥	617,347	3,029	62.9	.62:1
8♦ 7♠	379,624	3,029	38.1	1.62:1

Freed from being dominated in suit, 8-7 now figured to win as many flush hands as A-K. Because it will take a four-card flush on board to complete either competitor's flush, that freedom wasn't worth too much — about a one-half of one percent increase to be exact.

While each card was a different suit in the previous analysis, this time each of the two competing hands was a different suit. This was done by matching A♠ K♠ against 8♦ 7♦. Not only was 8-7 completely free from domination in suit by A-K, this time it would make more flushes. After all, it's much easier to make a flush with two suited cards than one. Take a look at the results.

Hand	Wins	Ties	Winning Percentage	Odds
Each hand a different suit				
A♠ K♠	605,114	4,349	60.7	.65:1
8♦ 7♦	390,537	4,349	39.3	1.6:1

This confrontation resulted in 390,537 victories for 8-7, a gain of 1.2 percent from the previous scenario, and nearly three percent better than the first scenario — when 8-7 was completely dominated in suit by Big Slick. This scenario is similar to the preceding one in that each hand will win all of its flushes, but there is a significant difference too. With two suited cards the chances of actually making a flush are much improved. This favors 8-7 over A-K because the weaker hand often needs a flush to win. Big Slick, on the other hand, will win most of the time without regard to whether it makes a flush. Because some of the flushes made by Big Slick are redundant — after all, it will win on its own merits any time the lesser hand does not improve — anything that equally increases each hand's chances of making a big hand is really a help to the weaker holding. Nevertheless, it's worth bearing in mind that some of these flushes were made by catching two running cards, or made with the hot breath of big overcards bearing down on the lowly 8-7, and these are hands that are usually thrown away in real games.

In the fifth analysis, we gave 8-7 as big an advantage as possible. This time 8-7 was suited, while Big Slick was both off suit and differently suited than 8-7. Even if a four-card flush came on the river, any flush made by 8-7 was guaranteed to hold up. Here are the results.

Hand	Wins	Ties	Winning Percentage	Odds
8-7 suited, A-K offsuit				
A♠ K♦	579,678	3,824	58.2	.72:1
8♥ 7♥	416,498	3,824	41.8	1.4:1

With the flush advantage squarely in the corner of 8-7, it fared better, improving by some 26,000 wins. This time, over the course of one million hands, 8-7 won nearly 42 percent of the time. It's an improvement, to be sure, although the hand is still a fairly significant underdog to A-K.

Now it's time to look at a full game. No more of this heads-up stuff. These scenarios are nine handed. Our two primary opponents are still A-K and 8-7, and this time each hand is double suited. In addition, seven randomly dealt hands were used to season the stew.

Hand	Wins	Ties	Winning Percentage	Odds
9 Players: each hand double suited				
A♠ K♠	223,113	3,162	23.2	3.3:1
8♦ 7♦	137,677	4,646	14.8	5.8:1
7 random hands			62	

With more opponents, the winning percentage of both A-K and 8-7 can be expected to drop considerably, and they did. This time A♠ K♠ won 223,113 hands —a winning percentage of 23.2 — while 8♦ 7♦ won 137,677 of the confrontations, for a winning rate of 14.8 percent. It's worth bearing in mind that with nine players active until the end of each hand, A-K is still guaranteed all of the flush wins in its suit, with the miniscule exception of straight flushes that may have been made by the random hands. On the other hand, 8-7 is not as lucky, and is much more likely to have some of its flushes trumped by bigger flushes made by random opponents.

Thus far, we've matched 8-7 against A-K. While A-K can grow into a big hand, it is a drawing hand nevertheless, and frequently needs some help from the flop. But what about a big hand, as opposed to a big *drawing* hand? To take this question out of the realm of the rhetorical, one final simulation was conducted. This time 8♣ 7♣ was pitted against a pair of aces. To give 8♣ 7♣ the best possible chance to strut its stuff, neither of the aces was a club.

Hand	Wins	Ties	Winning Percentage	Odds
8/7 suited vs. pair of aces				
A♠ A♦	335,516		33.8	2:01
8♣ 7♣	123,938		13.3	6.5:1
7 random hands			52.9	

As you probably surmised, a pair of aces is a much better hand than A-K, and it proved its merit by winning more than one-third of the confrontations. In a similar scenario, A-K was able to win only twenty-three percent of the time.

Nevertheless, 8-7 didn't fare that much worse against a pair of aces than it did against A-K, winning 13.3 percent of the time against a pair of aces and seven random hands as compared to 14.8 percent of the time against Big Slick and the seven dwarves.

The message here is threefold. Whenever a hand like 8-7 improves to a big hand, it can trump a pair of aces almost as frequently as it can beat Big Slick. When it does not improve at all it is always going to lose. When both hands improve to the same degree, 8-7 will also lose. To beat A-K, the board has to help the smaller hand and ignore Big Slick. To beat a pair of aces, the communal cards have to hit 8-7 twice.

The pair of aces really did its damage against the random hands. Those seven random hands, taken together, won sixty-two percent of the confrontations against Big Slick, as compared to only fifty-three percent when facing a pair of aces. That's food for thought if you suspect you're up against an opponent holding a big pair and are still of the opinion that any two cards can win.

There are a number of messages here. From these analyses, it's clear that mid-range suited hands do have value, and are always better than random holdings since they have the potential to occasionally grow into very big hands.

But in real poker they will not win as often as they will in the sterile and theoretical environment of a cold simulation, since players who have been dealt hands like 8♥ 7♥ will be much more prone to throw them in the muck when the flop doesn't help them and they are confronted with communal overcards and any appreciable action in front of them.

Since the mid-range suited connectors didn't do all that much worse against a pair of aces than they fared against Big Slick, it really validates their play in pot limit and no-limit poker — games in which one big pot with a well-disguised hand can make up for a plethora of one-bet calls and a mucked hand when the flop is anything less than miraculous.

Take these cold simulations for what they are: simple indicators of the inherent strength of a given hand, and not a model of real poker under real game conditions. And if you play and lose against a bigger hand when you believe you should have won, just because you were dealt 8♠ 7♠, you can always run from the table screaming, "… but they were soooooooted!"

Maybe one or two of your opponents will even sympathize with you. Most won't care. But in response to your ranting that a hand lik 8-7 suited should always win, a few might whisper the words that all poker pundits are prone to offer as universal words of sage advice, "It depends!"

Chapter 14

How to Play in Jackpot Games

$\textbf{H}$ave you heard this before? "… I just can't beat jackpot games!" Jackpot poker is an enigma. While the majority seem to love them, jackpot games always seem to leave players bemoaning their fate. "I can't beat these games," I've heard them say. "There are so many bad players, my good hands just don't hold up!"

In spite of such protestations, jackpot games are extremely popular. Jackpots of $20,000 or more have been common in Southern California. When there's a special promotion, like triple jackpots during Monday Night Football, a few lucky players have hit huge payoffs. During these promotions I have seen players who regularly play $30–$60 hold'em drop down to play in the $6–$12 jackpot game. The promise of immense overlays have caused these games to explode in popularity — often to the detriment of the $10–$20, $15–$30, or larger games.

Since you may occasionally play jackpot poker, we will examine these games and determine if they require any special strategic adjustments. We'll also lay to rest the adage that they can't be beaten. The truth is, they can be beaten. Players beat these games every day. Let's see how.

Does it Cost More to Play in a Jackpot Game?
Because money to fund the jackpot payout comes from player antes or blinds, it does cost more to sit in a jackpot game than it would in a non-jackpot game. Jackpot players, however, tend to call with more hands. Why? Because jackpot players, in essence, are playing two games simultaneously. Not only are they trying to capture the pot in front of them, they are also hoping for a windfall pot of gold at the end of the rainbow.

Your Opponents Will Probably Play Much Looser
When you're in a jackpot game, players have a tendency to play any pair, regardless of position. Why, for instance, would someone play a pair of deuces under the gun, with six players yet to act? Simple. The chances of making four deuces are exactly the same

as making any four-of-a-kind. And to participate in a jackpot, you've got to be in a hand where aces full, or better, is beaten. In most card casinos, both cards have to play.

Many players also cling to any straight flush combination, in a longshot attempt to hit it big. But some jackpot players are not in the game solely to hit a lottery-type longshot. They want to win, too, and they grow frustrated because they are constantly being drawn out on; hands which they believe should hold up get beaten with maddening regularity.

Making Adjustments

While some adjustments are required to be successful in jackpot games, it's important to point out that the game is still poker. You still have to make decisions designed to take advantage of the odds the pot offers when compared with the odds against making your hand. The essential nature of the game remains unchanged.

Just because someone runs down your pair of jacks with a 9–6 off-suit is no reason to adopt an any-two-cards-can-win attitude. But that's precisely what seems to happen to otherwise good players when they play in a jackpot game. A few bad beats and they start to play as poorly as their opponents — and sometimes worse.

If you're going to play in a jackpot game, here are some of the strategic adjustments I recommend.

First, understand that with more players in each pot, you're going to get beaten by lesser starting hands — simply because there are more of them out there against you. Second, because there are more opponents in each hand, you have to adjust the way you value certain hands.

Limit the Field With Big Pairs

If you're early to act with any big pair and someone has bet, you must raise. It is not an option. It is critical to limit the number of players against you. Pairs play better against fewer opponents. If you've got a big pair and the pot is raised in front of you, then reraise. Once again, you must attempt to limit the field.

If you're holding a big pair on or next to the button, and five or six players are already in the pot, your raise will most assuredly fail to convince any of them to fold. By raising under these circumstances, you're hoping to flop a set that might win a huge pot. Now your purpose in raising is to get more money in the pot, not to thin the field.

Once the flop comes, with so many opponents playing who-knows-what, it also becomes difficult to put a player on a hand. Any board card that does not specifically help you most likely helps one of your opponents. When three rags fall on the flop, don't be surprised to see your overpair raised by a small set or two small pair. Even if that player cold-called a raise with a pair of threes and flopped a set, don't be shocked. If you're making the proper adjustments for a jackpot game, you're going to be throwing away a lot of good-looking hands after the flop.

Good Draws are More Valuable

Hands that play well against a large field, such as high suited connectors, can make a lot of money. Although most of the time you're not going to be helped by the flop, when you do hit your hand you're likely to get a lot of calls. You will also rake in a nice pot.

Expect Big Swings

Expect bigger swings in jackpot games. When you win, you'll rake in larger pots. But your winning hands will be spaced farther apart. In statistical terms, the standard deviation will be larger. Much larger. You'll experience prolonged losses, only to recoup them quickly by raking in a pot which is bigger than it would have been in a non-jackpot game.

When you get right down to it, a jackpot game is not much different than a loose, non-jackpot game, with lots of players in each hand. Pairs and big cards go down in value. Good flush and straight draws increase in value, and can be played aggressively. If you hold A♥ 9♥, and two hearts fall on the flop, go ahead and bet — or raise — as long as you've got a lot of callers who figure to stick around and pay you off if you make the nut flush.

With many players in each hand, mid-range pairs usually have value only when a set is flopped. But, even when you do, be careful. Players will be sticking around with backdoor draws to flushes and straights or there might even be a bigger set out than yours.

Players who lose in jackpot games, but believe they should be able to beat the game, invariably have a difficult time releasing hands that do well in games with few callers. To succeed in jackpot games, you have to be able to release a hand, even one that may have looked like a winner before the flop.

Overcoming the Jackpot Drop

Players frequently ask the question, "How can I win in a jackpot game when so much money is raked from each pot?" They are referring to the additional amount that is dropped to fund the jackpot. While I can't prove this mathematically, I believe that the added number of players in each hand — coupled with the fact that players tend to stick around and pay you off when you have a winning hand — make it possible to overcome the jackpot drop. To overcome it, however, you must resist the trap of playing jackpot poker like it's a lottery. If you go too far with your hands in an attempt to either win the jackpot or catch a miracle card, you are probably giving away too much money.

But if you play a solid game, and make adjustments to account for the differing value of hands in a jackpot game, you should be able to overcome the jackpot drop. Let hitting the jackpot take care of itself — if it happens, it happens. However, you'll need discipline to avoid going on tilt after the bad beats you're sure to encounter in a game with a high degree of fluctuation, and also to avoid letting your more pedestrian opponents pull your play down to their level.

Chapter 15

Starting Standards

... The Gospel for Beginners, A Guide for Skilled Players, and a Point of Departure for Experts

One of the more enduring discussions among hold'em players at all levels — but particularly among beginning players — deals with starting standards. What kind of starting hands should be played is always a hot topic on the Internet newsgroup, Rec.Gambling.Poker, as well as in card casino conversations at and away from the table.

A lot of thought and quite a bit of research has historically been invested in this topic: After all, isn't each and every one of us looking for those hands that are guaranteed to be profitable in the long run, and aren't we equally interested in avoiding starting hands that are long-term losers?

Many poker pundits have developed guidelines for players to follow in determining which hands are playable from beginning, middle, or late position, under certain game conditions — such as the relative passivity or aggressiveness of a given game, whether it's a full game or short-handed, and how well one plays compared to one's adversaries. You could argue until the proverbial cows come home about which sets of starting standards are better, but it's not really worthwhile.

Most are similar, and in any event, there are no contrarian theorists out there arguing that you ought to play 9-2 offsuit under the gun. What's important is the simple fact that one ought to be following *some* set of standards. After all, everyone's standards come with the caveat that they should be modified based on position, and the texture of the game — and it's that elusive game texture that can neither be measured nor subsumed within a formula. And therein lies the rub. While you have to make adjustments to starting standards because of game texture, you're seldom certain whether your adjustments are correct. That's why a computer will never be able to play poker perfectly, and that's why — as long as your opponents are human — you'll seldom be certain that your adjustments are precise, accurate, and on the money.

That, however, doesn't negate the need for standards. Neither does the fact that your last three pairs of aces and kings were cracked by guys who stuck around to catch two runners and wound up beating you. Don't blame your starting standards for this; they're not at fault. Getting drawn out on has nothing to do with starting standards; it's about predicting the future — and there's precious little wisdom anyone can offer you on that topic.

But I can offer you some words of wisdom about playable hands: Starting standards should be the gospel for beginners, a guide for skilled players, and a point of departure for experts.

Simple? Of course it is. Still, some amplification is required. If you are a beginner, you shouldn't think about departing from whatever starting standards you adopt. Here's why. You will never deviate from starting standards because they are wrong. They're not. Once you know enough about the game to recognize appropriate opportunities, you can deviate because your adjustment represents a more profitable play. It doesn't obviate the book play, it simply means that for a specific situation, you've found an even more profitable alternative.

If you're a beginner or purely recreational player, you probably won't recognize those opportunities, and if you deviate from the book play, you'll be wrong more often than not. For a beginner, playing correctly will result in some very repetitive play on your part precisely because I'm suggesting that you follow these standards like a robot. In the long run, however, you'll be far better off than you'd be by looking for reasons to deviate from the book move. If you are a beginning or recreational player, be boring, be predictable, but build a foundation based on sound play, and you'll probably win money.

Once you have your chops down and know them cold, you can feel free to experiment. But please heed this word of caution. Experiment a whole lot less than you'd like to. Remember, most of the time the book move is the best move. That's why it's the book move. Stick with it most of the time.

Even chess masters play standard openings most of the time. They do it because it works. If you're a skilled player you can use standard play as a guide, rather than treating it as the gospel. Nevertheless, most of the time you'll still be playing book hands — only you'll be deviating just enough to put some variety into your game and some doubt into the minds of your opponents. Of course, this presupposes that your opponent is the type who pays attention to the kind of hands you're playing. If he's not, don't waste your time trying to deceive him. Just play straight ahead poker. You'll probably have to show down the best hand to get the money against this kind of adversary, but that has a bright side too. You won't have to waste any time or lose any money trying to be clever. Just come correct and you are guaranteed to win as long as you catch your share of good cards.

Even when you reach the exalted *expert player* level, you'll still play the right cards most of the time. The very fact that experts know all the book moves cold allows them to depart from starting standards once in a while, depending on the game, the opponent, and current game conditions and texture. Believe me, when you see an expert player win a big pot with what appears for all the world to be a terrible starting hand — "My God, how could he have called from fourth position with one player already in and only a 7♠ 6♠ in his hand" — unless you have reason to believe otherwise, just assume he had a reason for making that play. However, if he makes this play routinely, or makes it when he shouldn't, he is probably not really much of an expert at all — except I his own mind.

If you are playing pot limit or no limit poker, deviating correctly from book starting standards becomes even more important. The reason is simple. You don't need to capture all that many pots to win a goodly amount of money. But to win a bundle, you usually have to trap one of your opponents for some big bets. In no limit and pot limit games — where your opponents are likely to be even more wary than they are in limit games — you often need to be deceptive to accomplish this. And sometimes the easiest way to practice deception is to allow your opponents to fool themselves. How does one accomplish this? By playing a strange hand every now and then, and playing it in a manner that causes your opponent to become completely convinced that you are holding something you're not.

But without knowing starting standards cold, you'll never be able to put together a cogent plan. And whenever you make a move at the poker table without much of a plan, you usually don't have much of a prayer either.

Chapter 16

All About Money Management

Old paradigms, like old soldiers, never die. Some never even fade away. They creep so far into our consciousness that we cease to critically evaluate them. Once people believed the Earth was flat and the Sun revolved around it. Some of us still knock wood, whistle by a graveyard, avoid walking under ladders, and believe black cats bring bad luck while we patiently await the next harmonic convergence.

Money Management: What is it?

Money management is one of the concepts that should have died long ago, but didn't. It's still the frequent subject of discussion in gaming literature.

"What," you may ask, "is money management?" Part of it, the upside, is based on the timeless adage, "Quit while you're ahead." Once you've won a predetermined amount, get up and leave the game a bit wealthier and a lot happier than when you walked in.

The downside tells you, "Set stop-loss limits." Once you've lost $500 at one session, for example, it's time to quit. "Give it up and go home," say the high priests of money management, "you won't make it back today. Come back tomorrow. Lady Luck cold-shouldered you, and you ought to know better than to chase your losses."

Does this make any sense? Is it correct to quit while you're ahead? Should you quit once you've lost some predetermined amount? If you quit when you're ahead, as well as when you're losing, do you only play when your results are banded between arbitrarily-established stop-loss and stop-win limits?

Even money management advocates acknowledge that a poker game never ends, and it makes no difference whether you play four hours today and four hours tomorrow, or just play eight hours today. If that's the case, what is the logic behind money management theories?

Does it Really Make Sense to Quit While You're Ahead?

Let's look at each money management component individually. Proponents of the quit while you're ahead theory say that quitting winners lets you take your profit out of the game, and that you should not give back money you've already won. Actually, this makes sense only if you decide to quit poker entirely. If you plan never to play again, and you're ahead in today's game, quitting does allow you to permanently put today's profit into your pocket.

But if you quit winners today and lose tomorrow, are you any worse off than if you simply played on and lost what you had won earlier in the session? The answer, quite obviously, is no. You're not worse off. Coming back tomorrow simply allows you to pocket those winnings for a few more hours.

What About Stop-Loss Limits?

The same logic applies to stop-loss theory. If you are losing and leave the game, ask yourself whether you plan to play tomorrow — or next week, for that matter. If you answer "yes," then ask yourself this, "Do you think you can win?" If you plan on playing again and believe you can beat the game, is there any real difference between quitting now or continuing to play today?

I don't think so. If the game is so tough that you don't think you can win, you shouldn't play in it at all. If you regularly play in a game where you are not a favorite, you can expect to go broke — and it makes absolutely no difference whether or not you practice money management. But if you are a favorite, it pays to keep playing, regardless of whether you are ahead or behind at any given moment.

All You Need to Know About Money Management

Here's the only facet of money management that's true. If the game is good and you are a favorite, continue to play. If the game is bad and you are an underdog, quit! Never mind whether you're winning or losing.

Of course, the game can be terrific and you may not be a favorite for any number of reasons unrelated to the relative difference between your skill level and that of your opponents. You may be tired; emotionally upset from an argument with your spouse, kids, or boss; physically ill and not able to concentrate; or stressed out from work, traffic congestion, or any other threat to the sanctity of the human condition that might put you off your best game.

You will save yourself a lot of money over the course of your poker-playing career by following this simple rule: *If you're not playing up to your best abilities, go home.* The game will still be there tomorrow.

Game Selection and Money Management

Consider this. Gambling successfully is predicated on placing yourself in circumstances where you have a positive expectation. That's why there aren't any professional craps or roulette players. In the long run there is no chance of winning when insurmountable odds are stacked against you. You've chosen to play poker because you believe you can find games where you are favored over your opponents. While favorites do have losing nights, they show a profit in the long run.

Since one of the key concepts to winning at any form of poker is game selection, why would you voluntarily take yourself out of a good game, simply because you have won or lost some arbitrarily predetermined amount of money? Now I understand that if you've suffered a number of particularly insidious bad beats, and it's one of those nights that nothing seems to be going right, you might want to quit even though the game is good. That's OK, but only if you're quitting because you are no longer in the right frame of mind to continue playing to the best of your ability. Never quit just because you've reached a stop-loss limit.

What if you're in a good game and you're $1,000 ahead? Should you really quit when you're ahead? If the game is that good, and you have no other pressing commitments, why not go right on playing? After all, you're a favorite. Chances are you'll win even more money.

But whether you win or lose from that point on, your results were not predictable in advance. Your future results are always up for grabs, regardless of whether you keep playing now or pack it in. The game goes on, and the segments of time during which you're playing are only arbitrary delineations.

Summary

Here's the last word on money management. To paraphrase the poet John Keats, "That is all ye know on earth, and all ye need to know."

- Money management, as a strategy for maximizing winnings or limiting losses, is meaningless.

- Stop-loss limits, and quitting once you've won a predetermined amount of money, will neither stop your losses if you are a losing player nor protect your profits if you're ahead.

- Poor players will go broke no matter what they do. Good players will establish an expected hourly win rate regardless of whether they quit after they've pocketed a certain amount of winnings or keep playing.

- If you're playing in a good game, and are playing your best, stay in the game unless you have other obligations.

- If you're in a bad game, get out of it now — never mind whether you're winning or not.

- If you're emotionally upset, stressed out, fighting the flu, or otherwise not in your best condition, you're better off not playing.

Chapter 17

A Wholly Unremarkable Hand

Many of the hands discussed in print, and certainly the vast majority of hands players discuss among themselves, are remarkable because they possess certain unique qualities. We eagerly discuss the biggest pot we've ever won, the most unlikely draw-out, the time we flopped a straight flush and trapped six opponents for multiple bets, or that depressing twenty-two-to-one long shot that knocked us out of a tournament one spot away from the final table.

We don't, as a rule, invest much time or energy discussing unremarkable hands. They are certainly not the kind of stuff legend is made of, and while these unremarkable hands are quickly played and forgotten, they represent the vast majority of hands we play. Perhaps it's time to begin paying attention to them.

I was in fifth position, raised the blinds with A♥ Q♥, and was called by a player in seventh position. Everyone else folded, except the big blind, who called after pondering his hand. I loved the flop, It was Q♦ 7♠ 3♥. When the big blind checked, I came out betting. The player in seventh position called, and the big blind quietly folded. This was a situation I liked: heads up with top pair and top kicker, and no draw in sight.

The turn card was the 2♥. Not only did I have top pair with the very best kicker possible, I had a draw to the nut flush too. I bet. My opponent called. The river card was the 9♣, a complete blank. I didn't fear the board. It was Q♦ 7♠ 3♥ 2♥ 9♣. Neither straight nor flush was possible, and while I certainly did not have a lock on the pot, I came out betting. My opponent called and I showed my hand. As he flipped his cards toward the muck they turned face up, and I got a look at what he had played: It was J♦ 3♦. He called a raise cold with two suited cards that weren't worth much under any circumstances, and then called the flop with third pair and a backdoor flush draw. What's more, he kept calling, even when his rather remote flush possibilities disappeared entirely on the turn.

I was amazed, and while I've always assumed some people play this poorly — even in $20-$40 games — it's rather shocking to witness it first hand, with absolute certainty. In fact, this entirely unremarkable hand was an epiphany for me. In that moment I realized why poor players draw out on good players. Had my opponent been fortunate enough to catch two pair somewhere along the line, he would have won that pot, and I would have been left muttering to myself about a bad beat. Then I realized that my thinking was completely askew. Sure, players can, do, and will win hands occasionally when cold-calling a raise with holdings like J♦ 3♦. But even when they miraculously spin straw into gold like Rumplestiltskin, they don't do it very often, and certainly not frequently enough to turn a profit with hands like those.

This, I realized once again, is why certain players win money regularly, while other lose much of the time. "Most of the money you win comes not from the brilliance of your own play," I've written on more than one occasion, "but from the stupidity of your opponents." And here was a living, breathing example: a player who continued to call with the odds overwhelmingly against him. Yet call he did, in what would have been just another unremarkable hand — betting and winning a modest pot with the best hand, not high drama by any means — if my opponent did not accidentally expose his cards in the process of discarding them.

This epiphany was the realization that what I had long espoused was truer in all likelihood than I imagined. Hands like these are dull, gray, unremembered, and yet probably comprise the majority of our winning hands. We don't get rich off of solid, tough opponents. Poor players — who are more likely to draw out on us simply because they play so many hands and play them so poorly — contribute the vast majority of our winnings. The strange thing about this phenomenon is that we remember these poor players more for the few times they get lucky and beat us with horrid holdings than we do for all the unremarkable hands we win, but quickly forget, because nothing memorable, dramatic, or unusual took place.

There are lessons galore in this unremarkable hand. First and foremost is that old adage about game selection. If you have a choice of games, find one with the weakest players, particularly those who are prone to call too much, yet raise infrequently. This is the most desirable of all games. Even if you are not having a good run of cards you will usually win against this kind of lineup. In addition, because those players are so passive, you are not putting nearly the money at risk that you do in a game filled with aggressive players.

Second, don't whine about bad beats. If someone is going to play like my opponent and continue to call with nearly helpless hands, you ought to do everything in your power to sit in his game, even if he's beating you.

Third, most of your money will come from those boring wins you can't recall. While you will win the occasional monstrous pot — where it was capped before and on the flop and your A♠ K♠ gets lucky and makes the nut flush on the river, and your heart was palpitating the entire way as chips tumble into the pot like roadside gravel down a slippery embankment — it does not happen very frequently. Most of the money you win probably comes in a wholly unremarkable fashion. You start with the best cards, make the best hand, bet all the way, show down your hand, and win.

That's how it's supposed to happen. And in the final analysis, that's why it is not the least bit memorable. When all goes according to form — just as we expect — it doesn't even raise a blip on our radar. At the end of the day we've probably neglected the most important and significant events in our poker game. We won most of our money in a mundane and workmanlike fashion, from weak players who made a series of poor decisions. The lesson is simple. Play well. You'll win.

Chapter 18

Big Hands and Big Payoffs

ig hands are not always big money makers, and that's often frustrating. This is particularly true in split pot games like Seven-Card Stud Eight-or-Better High-Low Split, and Omaha High-Low Split (mercifully abbreviated as 7-stud/8, and Omaha/8, respectively).

In these games, where the high and low hands split the pot as long as there is a qualifying low hand, it's possible to make very big hands that don't win very much money. Imagine being dealt three kings in 7-stud/8, catching a fourth king on the next card against one opponent who is obviously drawing for low. You can bet and raise at every opportunity and if your opponent is lucky enough to wind up with any kind of raggedy low hand whatsoever, all you'll wind up with is half of the antes as your net profit.

While scenarios like this are more common in split-pot games than in games like Texas hold'em, where the high hand wins all the money, you see examples of it all the time in hold'em games too. Sometimes you have such a big hand that nobody else has a prayer. An example of this might be a flop of A♣ A♦ 4♠ and you're lucky enough to have been dealt A♠ K♠. There are no flush or straight possibilities on the flop, and you've flopped top set with the best possible kicker and a backdoor flush draw to boot.

If someone bets you can raise comfortably, or just call quietly, planning to checkraise on the turn — when the betting limits double. But you're not likely to get much action. After all, there's not much out there that anyone else could have. While it's possible that an opponent could be holding a pair of fours and was fortunate enough to flop a full house, that's not too likely. And even if he has, a running pair, the fourth ace, or any of the three remaining kings on the turn or river will make quick work of him.

But let's forget about the slim chance that your opponent flopped a full house. Most of the time your opponents will fold when you bet. If you are really fortunate, one of your opponents might try to steal the pot on the turn if everyone checks the flop. But he will probably fold when you raise. This, of course, allows you to gain a bet because your opponent — unaware that you flopped a huge hand — has tried to steal the pot.

But if none of your opponents try to steal the pot by betting into a board that portends a big hand, you're likely to be the one who bets and wins a small pot because no one else has enough of a hand — or even enough of a draw — to call. This is one of those situations where your opponents are all thinking, "Even if he is bluffing, he probably has the best hand."

So what's the lesson here? Aside from the realization that big hands do not necessarily lead to big pots, there are a number of things worth bearing in mind. First and foremost, it's important to realize that in poker — as in so much of life — all is relative. You don't have to have a huge hand to win, just one that's better than whatever your opponents are holding. Determining when you have the best hand is often as much an art as a science, and the ability to read the competition is one of the skills that top players have plenty of, and lesser players seem to lack altogether.

Some players are mesmerized whenever they make a good hand, even if they know deep in their heart that it's not the best hand and ought to be released. While it should be obvious to one and all that a bet saved is worth as much as a bet won, it seems difficult for many players to release losing hands, so they make costly crying calls again and again.

Winning a tiny pot with a huge hand is also a major source of frustration for many players. After all, one does not usually get all that many big hands in any given session, and when those big hands garner meager pots, it can be very frustrating. Not only is that galling, but the sense of frustration is inevitably exacerbated when someone else wins a fairly big pot on the next deal or the one after that with a relatively puny holding.

This is not unusual. You've probably seen players win small pots with big hands and become so unnerved because the payoff doesn't match what they believed they should have won, that they go on tilt and give it all back and more.

Whenever you flop a very big hand and do get some callers, you can probably bet the river with impunity as long as that last card cannot make an open-ended straight, a flush, or a full house. If an opponent is going to raise, chances are he'll do it on the turn. If you've got a big hand and your opponent simply calls the turn, you can bet and expect a simple call on the river unless it happens to be a real miracle card, or a card that makes a straight or flush a distinct possibility.

You don't have this latitude with smaller hands, like one pair. You might suspect yours is the best hand, but frequently you're just not sure.　As a result, checking the river is frequently the preferred course of action.

To make money with a big hand, at least one of your opponents has to have something too. That *something* might be a set, top two pair, or a draw to a straight or flush. If you flop or turn a big hand and get action, you have to do more than revel in the glory of whatever you might be holding. You have to determine whether you have the best hand. It's shocking how many players never look beyond their holdings, and that can produce costly mistakes. If you are driving a hand when your feet ought to be firmly planted on the brakes, it can cost three or four bets that might have been saved by considering the *relative* merit of your hand — rather than its absolute value.

Next time you find yourself holding a big hand, count your blessings if you win the pot, and if you find that you're getting a bit more action than you expected, take it for what it is: a flashing yellow light that says "Caution, danger ahead."

J ohn and I were seated at an empty table at Hawaiian Gardens, looking over the games and discussing various players at the tables nearby. "You see the guy over there in seat six?" I said, angling my eyes in that direction. "He calls anything and everything and raises with any two cards. That guy is really live." I went on to mention how I had raised on the button with K♥ J♥, and again on the flop when he came out betting. The flop was K-J-4 of mixed suits, and in my mind I was already stacking those chips. But the turn brought a six and the river card was an eight. My opponent showed 7-5 for a straight, and he was the one who was stacking the chips — not me.

"That's nothing," John said. "I saw him call a raise before the flop with nothing more than an unsuited four and a deuce, and the flop was no help whatsoever. But he caught two running deuces and his trips won a big pot."

Despite his recent good fortune, it was easy to see that the subject of our conversation was a losing player. "You don't see his cards all those times he calls and calls and finally mucks his hand on the river," John said. "What's more, you don't even remember those hands because they're insignificant. There's no bad beat, and no miracle card on the river. He'll just keep calling — or raising — until he finally mucks the losing hand. Most of the time his hands play out just like they should. It's the miracle catches that stick in our minds.

"I call them 'mystery chips'," John said. "You don't know where they come from, you don't know where he gets the money to buy them, and you don't even realize you're winning more chips than usual. A few additional chips just show up in every pot he plays — chips that you'd never win if a solid player folded those weak hands he's fond of playing — but they do accumulate."

John was right, of course. But he might even have underestimated just how rapidly those mystery chips add up. After all, our hero was playing almost every hand. Even if we err on the side of caution and estimate that he played only two-thirds of them — and it certainly seemed like it was more than that — those mystery chips rapidly accumulate. He was contributing $120 to each $20 - $40 hold'em hand he played all the way to the bitter end, and that's a conservative estimate. Since he was raising much of the time, his contributions were actually more than that. Even if one wins just a single pot per hour that our hero played, but really shouldn't have based on any reasonable criteria for hand selection, that's a lot of extra money at the end of the day. It's certainly enough to turn what might otherwise have been a breakeven session into a nice win.

Sometimes our hero is lucky and wins. Occasionally he'll even get extraordinarily lucky and book a *big* win. Don't worry about it. It's what keeps him coming back. After all, if he never won, how long do you think he'd subject himself to the indignities of losing day after day, week after week, and year after year?

Any winning session, regardless of how infrequently it comes about, provides our hero with all the rationale he needs to delude himself into deflecting his inadequacies elsewhere. He can blame his losing sessions on the cards, the dealers, or a sequence of what he would consider improbable and highly unlikely bad beats. None of that matters. What's important is that an occasional win provides all the rationale bad players need to persist in their losing ways, and to keep coming back for more.

There's no reason to feel as though the fates have conspired against you anytime a weak player has a winning day at your expense. It isn't personal. It's just the firm of *Probability Incorporated* conducting business as usual. And don't worry about those chips your opponent is stacking up. That money isn't really his. It's just visiting.

I suppose one of the morals of this story is to look for mystery chips whenever you can, and to capitalize on opportunities presented by players who persist in making *poker's Mistake Number One:* They call when they should have folded.

But that's not the only lesson to be learned here. When you think about all the mystery chips weak players contribute to poker games, the obvious conclusion is that it does not take all that many bad players to make a good game. Even one will do. Two weak players can be heaven on earth, even if all the rest of your opponents are outstanding players.

In Chapter 3 you saw the results of some simulations employed to study 30 years of poker — to see how much of one's results could be attributed to luck over the course of a lifetime of play. Using the same player profile in each seat of a simulated game, it appeared that approximately one to one-and-one-half percent of a player's life-long results might be attributable to luck.

This simulation was repeated after substituting one player who called too often and another who played too tight for two of the otherwise identical player profiles. The results were astonishing: Mr. Rock was a significant loser and Loose Lee lost even more; it was a staggering amount of money. And these profiles played significantly better than our hero with the mystery chips.

The empirical evidence is very clear, and supports what one sees in poker games every day. It does not take all that many poor players to make for a good game. One or two is enough. Not only are they enough, they'll more than negate the fact that others in the game might have abilities that exceed yours. After all, most of the money won comes not from the brilliance of your own play, but from the poor play of your opponents. And that's no mystery at all.

Chapter 20

Once you've learned poker's strategic concepts, and have played long enough to develop a feel for the game's pace and texture, you can become an excellent poker player in the wink of an eye … in an instant.… in a nanosecond. Just like that, and in less time than it took you to read from there to here.

Does this sound like an offer from another self-improvement huckster? Isn't excellence a long time in the making? No. You can do it right now. It's the real deal. Here's how you can accomplish this wondrous feat. Like the Nike commercials admonish us, *Just do it!*

Commit to it

Make the commitment, and it's done. Then, work your tail off every day for the rest of your life to make sure it stays done. IBM founder Thomas Watson said, "If you want to achieve excellence, you can get there today. As of this second, quit doing less-than-excellent stuff." Sound simple? Sure, but like the Golden Rule, most profound truths are simple.

Zero Tilt Factor

A poker theorist once wrote about having "… a zero tilt factor." A seemingly simple statement that is really quite profound. Zero tilt factor is nothing more than a commitment we choose to make that will account for our poker success more than our technical knowledge.

Because his statement really touched a nerve in me, I consciously committed to zero tilt factor (or ZTF as I like to call it). I simply made a commitment that I would never go on tilt again. Not for one session, not for one hour, not even for one hand. This commitment alone gives me an extra edge over any player who occasionally goes on tilt. The money he throws off, I'll catch! How many of you can say the same thing about your own game — that you never go on tilt? Not sometimes, not occasionally, but *never*.

The key to excellence is making a commitment. Wishing or wanting to achieve excellence is not enough. Neither is it sufficient to merely involve yourself in an attempt for excellence. *You have to commit to it.* Make no bones about it, there is a significant difference between involvement and commitment. It's like the difference between ham and eggs. The chicken is involved; the ham is committed!

Want to be a great poker player? Commit to greatness. Sure, you won't be any better ten minutes after you've made that commitment than you are right now. But commitment is a necessary first step down a long road. You'll need to study poker. You'll need to think about the game while you're at the table and when you're away from it.

Go ahead and model your own game after players you respect. Talk to winning players you admire for the way they play. Keep on doing the things it takes to guarantee yourself the best of it. Excellence is a long quest and a never-ending journey — one you'll need to pursue until your deal is done.

Still, you can declare your excellence tonight, starting with the first hand you play. How do you begin? Visualize yourself as the greatest poker player ever — and act accordingly. Sound silly? Even embarrassing? It's not.

A few years before I began writing a regular column for Card Player, the instructor in a writing seminar told me, "The way to become a published writer is easy. Just put on the hat of a writer, and you'll grow into it!"

Just do it. And you know what? It works. So does the adage which says, "Ninety percent of success is just showing up." That's what this is all about, *showing up* — and showing up every time you play for the rest of your competitive life. Commitment — that unbreakable bond to excellence, while easily made, carries with it this mandate: I will picture myself as the greatest poker player ever, and always play accordingly.

Sure, you'll slide through valleys on your road to the heights. So what! Life is not a kindergarten, and most things worthwhile do not come without having to endure struggle and adversity.

Do it Now!

Here's a terrific opportunity. When you sit in your next game, play like an excellent player. Don't delude yourself into playing a less-than-quality hand because you "...have a feeling." Don't play tired, and don't take the worst of it. Make the plays a top player would. You already know much of what they do. You only need to apply it, and apply it every time you sit in a game. Never, but never, permit yourself to play less than your best. That's what commitment is all about. That's one of the implications behind the decision you make in the wink of an eye.

If you don't know what a top player would do in a given situation, it presents an opportunity for you to learn. To keep your commitment you need to learn something new every day. And once you learn it, go out and practice it. Making that commitment, and once having decided to do what it takes to achieve excellence as a poker player, never do anything, no matter how trivial, inconsistent with your commitment.

Here's the truth, and it's simple. It does not take long to make changes. It takes forever to maintain change, but changes of the most dramatic, fundamental, and far-reaching kind can be had instantly. It's true with diets, smoking, and becoming a great poker player. Want to quit smoking? Just give up cigarettes! Want to lose weight? Don't eat any fats and exercise aerobically for thirty minutes every day! It will work for you when you work at it. Want to be a better poker player? Commit to playing better. Just do it.

It's All or Nothing

But remember, it's all-or-nothing. You either commit to making change or you don't. Saying you're going to change, and then doing it all except for five or six weak hands you decided to play because you were tired, or had a hunch, just doesn't cut it. You're either there or you're not — you're on the bus or off the bus. No in-betweens allowed. This is a bet you can't hedge.

You want to be a top-notch poker player? Great. Go ahead and commit to it. Do it and it's done. You can reach excellence in a heartbeat, and you can do it today. But if you do, there will be no more talk about bad beats, or that dealer who kills you. Once you commit to achieving excellence and being the best poker player alive, you can never again place the blame for your failures or fortune on anyone else. Your results are your own. You own them and they belong to you.

And if you decide not to make that commitment, it's no big deal. Just recognize the truth for what it is. You're a recreational player who cares more about enjoyment than results. Nothing wrong with that, but you can't have it both ways. If you want to be a winning, excellent player, go ahead and do it. It takes no time at all to achieve change, but it will take forever to maintain it. *It's that simple.* Really.

Chapter 21

My good friend Paul Zibits outplayed 233 others to finish seventh in the 1999 World Series of Poker's $2,500 buy-in, hold'em tournament. That's not bad when you stop to think about it, pocketing nearly $15,000 for two days work. But plenty of players finish in the money each year, and "What," you may wonder, "is so unusual about Zibits' seventh-place finish?"

Actually, nothing was unusual about his finish. What was unusual is that Paul Zibits — by profession a bassist with the Pacific Symphony Orchestra in Orange County who also performs on numerous movie and TV soundtracks — has been playing poker for just three years. In that short time he's progressed from novice to tough tournament veteran, as well as a consistent winner in Southern California's cash games.

I measure Paul's poker growth by the age of his son, Zachary. We met when Paul was just embarking on his quest to learn poker. Our friendship began as a correspondence, when he wrote to ask me some questions about poker strategy. Since we both live in Long Beach, we decided to meet for lunch at a local restaurant near the pier. Paul was frazzled when he walked in, looking for all the world like a guy who had been up all night playing poker. "My wife's in the hospital," he said by way of introduction, "she had a baby last night." I was shocked that he hadn't canceled our meeting. Then I realized that anybody who can set aside the birth of his son for a few hours to discuss poker was obviously serious about learning the game.

During lunch Paul told me about the storied tradition of poker and classical music, explaining that one of the longest running poker games in the world is the one played at New York's Metropolitan Opera. It has been going steadily for 118 years, even outlasting two opera houses. The game is played in the musicians lounge between rehearsals and performances, and even travels with the company. During the first half of the century, the game was played on the train between cities when the Met was on tour.

Research scientists have long known the parallels between music and mathematical aptitude, but there are deeper ties. Paul tells me that becoming a good poker player is much like becoming a good musician. "First you must master a large amount of technique. In a musical instrument it is scales and positions, and then playing etudes. In poker, it is learning when to bet certain hands, your position at the table, and which hands to raise.

"Once you learn the technique," Zibits said, "there is the larger art form to master. You make a musical interpretation from the notes, and in poker you learn how to read your opponent. Poker is a game of incomplete information. You must fill in the missing pieces. You do it with psychology and very close observation."

None of this is a secret, of course. But Zibits assimilated these lessons in three short years. Some players have been at the game for decades and have yet to master some of these essentials. How was he able to achieve this?

Paul Zibits learned poker the correct way. Not only did he play, he also studied. He read my books and every other poker book he could get his hands on. Then he played, and when something was not clear to him, he inquired. I'm not the only poker player Paul learned from. He also discussed poker theory and strategy with anyone he felt could impart the knowledge that would help him grow and mature as a player.

In so doing, he's been able to jump-start his poker career to the point where he is now an outstanding player — a consistent winner in cash games as well as a threat in any tournament he enters.

Regardless of whatever musical talent and aptitude Paul possesses, he would never have become the outstanding musician he is today without dedication and practice. And he applies that same discipline to poker. What's more, everyone reading these words can do it too. While Paul Zibits is now a terrific poker player as well as a gifted musician, he'd be the first to tell you that he is neither Stu Ungar nor Mozart — both wunderkinder with innate, almost mystical abilities that set them apart from others who are, by comparison, merely gifted.

Like the vast majority of us, Paul is workmanlike. Very few of us have Mozart's quotient of innate talent, or Ungar's seemingly uncanny ability to know the cards you were holding even before you did. But discipline takes no talent whatsoever. The only requirement is will power: a relentless drive to become better by focusing one's efforts on a goal and persevering until it is achieved. It's "March or die," and one either exerts the will to move forward, or runs the risk of being blown about by the wind somewhere along the way.

If you are new to poker, take heed in this. You can become a good, winning poker player in a relatively short period of time. It takes knowledge, experience gained at the tables, and a willingness to continue thinking critically about poker and a desire to learn something new about the game every day. Books, play, talking with players you respect, computers: all of these are tools at your disposal. Use them and you can become a much better player much more quickly than others who are so seduced by the action and thrills of the gamble and the game that they process little, if any, of the broadband stream of information that flows across the poker tables.

Paul Zibits went from novice to winning poker player in a few short years. Can anyone do it? I'm not sure, but I am certain that most beginning players can progress much more rapidly than they might suspect. The key lies in a comprehensive, integrated approach to learning the essentials of the game — and when those essentials are mastered, it is time to move to another level and play the game as though you have achieved a Zen-like state of instinctive awareness. Like most opportunities, it's not easy, but it's there for the taking.

Chapter 22

Cards and Cultures

his world is filled with cultural stereotypes. Some are social-
ly acceptable, others aren't. A few are ludicrous, while others blatantly contradict one another. Care for an example?
The English are reserved. That's a generalization to be sure, and
all one has to do is think about the behavior of two generations of
British rock musicians and a few English soccer hooligans to realize that if there is any truth to the myth of English reservation and
propriety, there are also a hell of a lot of exceptions.

Here in California there's a stereotype of immigrants suggesting
that they are lazy. There's an equally strong countervailing stereotype that depicts these very same immigrants as incredibly hard
workers, willing to toil long and hard at jobs most born-in-the-
USA Americans wouldn't think of doing, in order to send hard
earned dollars to support families they've left behind.

These stereotypes carry over to the poker table too. In Southern
California, where there's a large immigrant population, many
players view them as guys who like to gamble and shout unintel-
ligible phrases at the top of their lungs as they fire yet another raise
into the pot. It makes no difference to the beholder where these
players hail from; if their native tongue is not English they are generally viewed as action players.

Stereotyping of this sort and worse takes place at poker tables every day. In fact, not only do native-born Americans stereotype for-
eign-born players, they stereotype themselves too.

The guy with the tattoos and the biker gear is always viewed as a
degenerate gambler, while the guy in the suit, tie and wingtip
shoes is a rock. We even stereotype players based on geography.
Everyone knows that out in California we're all no-fold'em
Hold'em players, and that Nevada casinos are populated primarily
by rocks and stones, and a few grind-it-out pros, both of whom lay
in wait for fishy tourists.

Is there any truth in these assessments, and if so, what implication
does it have for playing strategies? I firmly believe that games in

California are looser than they are in Nevada, but economics — not cultural differences — lie at the root of this phenomenon. Southern California, where I play, is home to the music industry and the movie business, as well as agents, lawyers, managers, and all the others that hover about entertainment industry mega-dollars in a perpetual feeding frenzy.

Northern California is filed with dot.com millionaires — all those twenty-somethings who have struck it big by cashing in stock option from start-up companies that have created instant wealth through public offerings. When there's that much money floating around, some of it eventually filters into the card room. Since many of California's affluent really do have more money than they know what to do with, a lot of them like to gamble when they play poker.

Nevada players seem to play tighter than their counterparts in the Golden State. Many Las Vegas poker room habitués are retirees, on a fixed income, and their money is a lot dearer to them than it is to a movie mogul who can do a multi-million dollar deal whenever the coffers seem depleted, or to a dot.com dude who can peddle a few fifty-cent options for $200 a share anytime he's experiencing a bad run of cards.

I've noticed different playing styles elsewhere too, though I can't explain them as conveniently as the difference between Nevada and California playing styles. My very limited experience in Atlantic City suggested that Hold'em players there are similar to California players before the flop, but they tighten up significantly afterwards. If the flop wasn't favorable, most of the time the Atlantic City regulars I've played against were not at all reluctant to muck their hands.

Let's assume that there is some validity to different geographical playing styles. What should that mean to the average player? In California style no fold'em games you won't have much success bluffing your opponents, and you'll frequently have to show the best hand to win the pot. When players are more prone to stick around with all sorts of hands, it becomes difficult to determine if subsequent cards have helped your adversaries. Against opponents who play by the book, a rag is just that, while against no fold'em players that rag might just be a card that gives one of your opponents two pair or a set.

If you catch part of the flop in a no fold'em game, you have to bet or raise to make it as expensive as possible for your opponent — who is presumably taking the worst of it — to draw against you. The concept of semi-bluffing, where a bet will prove profitable in the long run because you have two ways to win — you might make your hand or your opponent might throw his away — is obviated in a game where no one folds. Players in games like these will experience much larger swings than their counterparts in more conservative games. With more players contesting each pot, even when some of them are long shots, you can be sure that you will be putting more of your money at risk. You should win more money in the long run, but the impact of a much higher variance may be too much for some players' bankrolls, not to mention their psyches.

When players are a bit more conservative, big cards go way up in value. With only a few players expected in each pot, a hand like A-K might win without improvement. Moreover, the holder might be able to drive opponents out of the pot who otherwise might have gotten lucky and drawn out on Big Slick.

This phenomenon has implications for starting hands too. In California, where family pots are not uncommon, one can win a great deal of money with a straight or flush. You almost always get the right price to draw for it. That's not always the case in tight games, when the money in the pot might not offset the odds against a draw, even when one is fortunate enough to make his hand.

My advice is to be careful about stereotyping — of any kind. It's sort of like swords, and those that live by the stereotype frequently die by it. By the same token, you'd be remiss if you failed to take notice of whether you're in a no fold'em game or a tight one, and neglected to adjust your strategy accordingly.

Chapter 23

The Desperate Hours

What are your desperate hours? Is there a time during each poker session when you don't play your best? Researchers have long known that people perform better at some times than others, and it varies from one person to the next. Some of us begin the day on a high note and are at our best early in the morning, but we run straight down from there. Others among us are night people, and hit our stride once the sun sets. Still others do well in the morning, lag in the middle of the day, but catch a second wind in the evening.

Poker players are no different. Some are at their best when they first sit down. It takes a while for others to get into the flow of the game. Although everyone's game tends to fall apart when they're tired, some of us can play all day before tiring while others run out of energy after six or seven hours at the table.

My own desperate hours occur when I first sit down. It always takes me a while — usually between 30 minutes and an hour — to get into the flow of the game. Unless I've had an opportunity to scope out the game from the rail while I'm waiting for a seat, I don't know who's on tilt, who's been calling every bet and raise with a weak hand, and I can't tell whether a player's raise represents a legitimately strong hand or is simply the actions of a maniac who's throwing money into the pot more out of habit and ego than anything else.

Oh sure, if the maniac is a regular player and usually plays that way, I won't necessarily credit him with a strong hand when he bets or raises, but even maniacs can go through cool-down phases between periods of intense, unrelenting, and frequently unwarranted aggression.

Not everyone plays the same way all the time. Even the same players in the same game go through periods of overvaluing and undervaluing their hands. And their change in playing style depends on a multitude of factors. If an aggressive player is getting beaten up it can mitigate his aggression. Even perpetual maniacs realize that losing diminishes the intimidating aspects of overly aggressive play. But not always. Sometimes a spate of bad cards and bad luck just leads to more aggression, and you never know which way your favorite maniac is tilting unless you're watching it happen.

Poker games sometimes seem like organic entities with lives of their own. They are a supple, dynamic medium with characteristics that change before your very eyes, even when the players remain the same. And it takes me a while to connect with that dynamic and plug into the game's texture so that I am accurately reading and reacting to the shifting sands and changing winds swirling around me.

When I first sit down in a game and get involved in a pot I have a tendency to stay too long with hands I should have abandoned — and would have, too — once all my antennae have been deployed and are working optimally.

The fact of the matter is this: the first hour I play can cost me money. Maybe I'm even a losing player for my entire lifetime of first hours. I don't know for sure, but I am bound and determined to do something about it.

Becoming aware of a problem is, of course, the first step towards solving it. Now that I'm aware of it, I'll be a bit more judicious when I first sit down in a game. Maybe I'll wind up leaving a little money on the table with hands I win, but I plan to lose my proclivity to call on those occasions when I should have folded during my first hour of play.

I have another desperate hour too — though it's not that much of an issue for me. It's when I'm tired. My antennae are deployed, all right, but they're working overtime. When I'm on overload I simply cannot process information as well as I can when I'm sharp and on top of my game. This, however, is no big deal for me. I generally get up and go home when I hit the wall. I beat down that old urge to stick around when I'm losing in hopes of getting even a long time ago.

But other players haven't, and I frequently have a box seat from which to watch their play slip by degree. Good players are not immune to this shortcoming either, and I'm not about to tell them — not at the table, anyway. The fact that I play much better once I've been in a game for an hour or so is a recent revelation for me. I never thought much about it before, and don't recall seeing much about it in print either — though I'm sure that somewhere, some other poker pundit happened on this a long time before I did. Nevertheless, this is a think piece for you as well as a confession of sorts for me. Ask yourself whether there's a particular time of day, or point in a playing session when you are vulnerable — and if there is, what can you do about it?

Do you throw off money out of euphoria when you win a couple of pots in a row? Does your playing style change appreciably when you are tired, and how long does it generally take until your energy begins to lag? What about when you first sit down in a game: Does it take you a while — as it does me — to get a read on your opponents and the texture of the game you're in?

Think about it. You might be able to plug up a leak in your game simply by recognizing your periods of vulnerability and playing cautiously until they pass. Until you do, take heed and remember Pogo's immortal words: "We have met the enemy and he is us."

Chapter 24

Computers and Hold'em

C omputer programs incorporating strategy seem to offer everything an aspiring poker student could want or even hope for. You can test your mettle against an entire table of computerized opponents programmed to play at a variety of skill levels while employing a wide spectrum of playing styles. Your computer can also be utilized as a tool to compare and assess the strength of one hand against a score of others. It can even conduct simulated studies can be conducted to determine whether you made the best decision in last night's game, by repeating your action thousands — or even millions — of times, and seeing how well it fares in the long run.

How Well Does Poker Software Play?

While computerized poker programs still do not possess the ability to play their opponents as well as real experts would — although impressive strides have been made since the first edition of this book was published — they are improving by leaps and bounds, and it's probably only a matter of time until good poker software will be able to compete at the highest levels. After all, it was once thought that no chess program could beat a top-notch grandmaster. But that was before IBM's "Big Blue" defeated none other than world champion Gary Kasparov, the highest rated player in chess history.

While there are significant differences between chess and poker — like reading tells by observing the mannerisms of one's opponents — don't be too surprised if poker software begins to compete at an exalted level in the foreseeable future.

A personal computer offers an opportunity to jump-start your poker progress by providing the opportunity to play against skilled computerized opponents while receiving advice from expert advisors who can be queried at any time during the play of a simulated hand. By studying study poker books and using a computer to practice your newfound skills, you can avoid the anguish and expense of gaining experience the old-fashioned way — losing your money in the school of hard knocks.

In addition to playing against computerized software, you can also ply your newly hatched skills against real opponents by playing on the Internet for real money — or for no money at all, in "free" games. You can use the Internet to simulate the experience you might have by playing in a real casino, though it's important to bear in mind that play in a real casino will require a period of adjustment, never mind how much experience you may have garnered in on-line, play-money games.

Surfing the Internet for Poker Information

The Internet newsgroup rec.gambling.poker is an open forum representing the entire poker community, from beginners to well-known experts — including more than a few players who have won the World Series of Poker. When you go online, you can also participate in the Internet Newsgroup, rec.gambling.poker (or "RGP" as it's called) as well as visit other poker sites where you can purchase books, videos, and software, read articles by experts, pick up information about tournaments and games you might want to enter, and even ask questions of well known poker experts.

RGP affords anyone with an interest in poker an opportunity to follow and participate in an ongoing on-line dialogue that will provide answers to your questions, as well as sharpen skills and increase your understanding of the game. Through e-mail, you'll be able to query expert players who participate in Newsgroup discussions.

Anyone can access this forum and read or respond to messages posted there, or address poker-related questions to the group. Whether you want an opinion about how to play a given hand, or where you might find a casino or home poker game in London, England, London, Ontario, or New London, Connecticut, the Internet newsgroup rec.gambling.poker is the place to find out. Someone who plays in one of those locations on a regular basis will supply you with all you need know to find a game wherever you are. If you play poker and want to find a game on your travels, you'll learn that's it's not such a lonely planet after all.

Any relatively up-to-date computer with the latest Windows operating system (you'll need a Windows operating system; the best poker software is not available for a Mac), a 56K modem, sound card, 64 megabytes of RAM, and a CD-ROM will suffice. If you are not a computer maven, ask a friend to help you select one. If you have to go it alone, just follow the ads in the Sunday paper and you'll see that computers meeting these specifications can be had at a very reasonable price.

Practicing Poker With Your Computer

Back in poker's dark ages, players learned only through the school of hard knocks. They belied up to the table, played poker, wagered their money, took their lumps, and if they were clever fellows who could learn quickly enough to exceed the speed at which their bankroll was wasting away, they stood a chance. That was it.

The coming of poker books made things a lot easier for those willing to study them. A continuous, iterative cycle of reading, studying, playing, and thinking critically about the game, gave players who studied poker as well as played it a real leg up on the competition.

Now your computer can function as a poker coach and instructor, while providing a variety of practice opponents for you to compete against. Best of all, there's no financial risk, and you'll continue to improve.

Turbo Texas Hold'em: State of the Art Software

Wilson Software's Turbo Texas Hold'em is the state of the art as far as poker software for Texas hold'em is concerned. If you want to broaden your horizons, Wilson Software also offers similar software for other commonly played poker games.

Your cyber opponents — with their ability to bluff and semi-bluff, slow play and checkraise, make adjustments for position and number of players, alter strategy when checkraised, and their ability to react to events in prior hands — are no slouches. They'll take their share of pots while preparing you for real games.

Another remarkable feature of this technology is it's research mode, which allows you to direct the computer to play 100,000 or even one-million simulated hands — the equivalent of somewhere between a full year's play and a lifetime of poker — in the time it takes you do eat dinner. Simulations are very high-speed tests in which the computer does all the playing so that you can learn something. If you want to test a tactical ploy of your very own, you can customize a player profile to mimic your playing style and load it into the lineup for your test. The computer plays out the scenario, and then presents you with a variety of game statistics. You'll know how much you won — or lost — to the penny.

How To Improve the State of the Art

In 1995, when the first edition of this book was published, I stated that if I had good skills as a programmer, I would improve the way computers simulate human poker playing skills by:

- Constructing programs that allow simulated players to track activities of their opponents, and make their own decisions accordingly. For example, if I constructed three players, one of which plays too tight and the other too loose, I'd like the third player (who plays correctly) to be able to recognize whether the raise is coming from the loose or tight player and adjust its play accordingly.

- Modifying programs to evaluate decisions made by other computerized players over the last 30 - 60 hands (a simulated half-hour to an hour) of play and adjust its own actions accordingly.

While 1995 might not seem like ancient history to most of us, it is positively the Middle Ages when measured against the rapidity of software development. *Turbo Texas Hold'em* now does all of this and more, and some of the player profiles can effectively determine if other profiles — as well as the human player in the game (that's you, buddy) — is playing well or is on tilt, blithely steaming his or her cyber chips away.

Although computerized poker strategy still lags behind chess software, it's improving at a rapid rate. While I wouldn't expect a piece of poker software to stand a chance of winning the World Series of Poker anytime soon, current programs play well enough to hold their own in many cash games in card clubs and casinos all over the world.

The Internet Casino: A 21st Century Phenomenon

Although the best poker books, videos, and software programs provide a solid framework for winning play, they do not provide the hands-on, interactive game experience every player needs to improve. A computer can also transport you via the Internet to play-money games in which you will compete against live opponents much like you; they just want to learn and have fun. Not only can you play against them, you'll also be able to "chat" as you play by typing messages back and forth on your keyboards. There's no cost other than a nominal fee for using the Internet site. And compared to the tuition at the school of hard knocks, it's a bargain.

When you feel confident enough to play for real money, there are a variety of Internet poker casinos where you can play against real people for real money! The only difference between these games and those in real casinos is that your opponents will not be seated at arm's length from you around a poker table. Instead, they could be located anywhere in the world, connected to you via a distinctly 21st Century technology: an Internet casino.

The Internet makes it easy to log on and jump into a real game against real opponents. There are play-money games, and games where real money changes hands. Poker in cyber casinos is offered at a variety of betting limits, just as it is in a real casino. While you can't hear your opponent's voice, or study his mannerisms, he can't study yours either. But you will see on the screen is a depiction of a poker table, with icons representing players and chips that move at great speed from each player's stacks into the pot and back again, when the pot is pushed to the winning player.

Even the play-money games will help a beginner improve as a player, since there is a significant difference between playing against a computerized program and a real opponent. Playing on-line will help any beginner learn to read the board, deduce what his opponent might be holding by studying his betting patterns, develop a sense of whether to check or bet, and whether to fold, call, raise, or reraise. On-line, play-money games are a terrific opportunity to familiarize oneself with common hold'em situations, such as flopping a straight or flush draw, and learning how to quickly assess whether the odds offered by the pot make it worthwhile for one to continue with a drawing hand.

It's easy enough to find these games in cyberspace. One can either search for online casinos, or simply go to the web sites shown on various poker links. In addition, many online casinos advertise regularly in *Card Player Magazine* and *Poker Digest*.

With the ability to harness, employ, learn, and improve one's poker using sophisticated software designed for this purpose, and the ability to use the Internet as a learning tool, it has become almost imperative for any serious player to utilize a computer for these purposes.

Chapter 25

Are You Ready to Play Professionally?

To most recreational poker players the idea of playing professionally seems like a dream. Get up when you want to, work when and where you choose, and ply your trade almost anywhere — from London to Las Vegas and California to Costa Rica, casino poker awaits you there. So what's stopping you? Only a positive answer to one very critical question, "Can I make a living doing this?"

Poker isn't like most jobs. For one thing, if you're a poker player, you won't have a steady salary coming in. Not only that, even commissioned salespeople won't lose money if they don't make a sale. But poker players can and do lose money whenever they have a bad day. It's one of the few jobs where you can go to work and cost yourself money. Imagine that. An entire day of poker — under stressful conditions — and all you've got to show for it is a couple of grand less than you started out with. Not a pretty picture, is it?

Still, people take up poker as a profession every day. Some do so after years of deliberation. Others pursue it as a second career — after retirement — when they have alternative sources of income to steady the ship in a storm. Others just dive in, like learning to swim by jumping off the edge of a dock. How successful are they? I don't have any statistics handy — I don't think anyone does — but I'd be willing to venture a guess that the majority of newly hatched professional poker players go broke, and probably do so within a year.

So how do you know if you can make a living playing poker? For a relatively unstable profession, there seem to be quite a few indices available to the seasoned player who's thinking about earning his living at the tables. Here are a few I'd recommend.

The first and most obvious factor to consider is your own results. Anyone seriously considering poker as a career needs to keep his or her poker diary up to date, and do it assiduously. Of course you'd prefer to avoid recording a big loss from that night you went on tilt. You were tired, just had a fight at home, were stuck in a traffic jam just getting to the casino, and of course you didn't play your best. Never mind all that. When you're playing for a living, no excuses are allowed. It's the school of hard knocks — where reality counts, and wouldda, shouldda, couldda doesn't mean a thing. Part of being a professional player is how well you play when you're not at your best — and you won't be bright-eyed all the time. But that's no reason not to play your best. You should play your best game every time you walk into a casino. If you don't feel you can, you shouldn't play. Remember, playing poker frees you from a time clock. You don't have to play. And if you're not up to par, it will cost you far less to go see a movie than it will to visit the tables.

If you haven't been keeping good records, you are not ready to play professionally. Oh, you can give it a go. No one's going to stop you. But without a foundation in data of your results, you might simply be deceiving yourself about your ability, and that can cost you more than money. If you have a career, a family, or other responsibilities, then going broke playing poker will take its toll on them all. If you don't believe me, just look around. Casinos are littered with broken souls and busted players.

But let's look at the bright side. Suppose you have been keeping good records, and what's more, you're a winning player. What should you do now? That's easy. You need to decide where you want to play for a living. Perhaps you are living in an area where there are only small limit games — too small to provide the kind of livelihood you want — and you decide to move to California, or Las Vegas, or Atlantic City, or even Europe, for that matter. Before you make the leap, do yourself a favor. Take the time to go there for at least a month to six weeks.

There might be a big difference between the games where you want to live and those in your own backyard. And if you're moving up to bigger limits because you can't earn a decent living in smaller games, you can be assured of one thing: As you move up the ladder, the players get better. Part of becoming a professional poker player is finding your niche in the food chain. It's a question of striking a balance between the betting limits, which have a major impact on how much money you *can* earn, and the quality of your opponents, which will have a huge impact on how much you *will* earn. Lower limit games are more easily beaten, but small limits constrain the amount of money you can expect to win. Big limit games generally have tougher players in the lineup. Somewhere, if you are good enough, there's a limit you can beat, and it offers the best balance between your theoretical earning power and your actual win rate. When you've found it, you've arrived. That's not to say you can't move up. But it is where you belong now — assuming you're trying to feed your wallet at the tables rather than your ego.

If you only think you can beat the games you intend to play for a living, but aren't certain, you can use statistics to help you get a handle on what you might expect to win over the long haul. This involves calculating your standard deviation — a measure of variability — and then using that measure to assess the kind of results you might achieve with some degree of reliability. Any book on statistics will show you how to calculate your standard deviation, and there's a simple arithmetic process for doing just that in Chapter 27 "For the Record" on page 152. But an even simpler way is to use your computer and a spreadsheet program like Microsoft Excel. If you don't own a computer any $20 pocket calculator with statistical functions will also enable you to accomplish this task.

Let's say that after 900 hours of playing $20 - 40 hold'em, your standard deviation is 20 small bets per hour, which is equivalent to $400. Everyone's standard deviation is different. Yours will depend on a number of factors, including your playing style, your opponents, and the relative passivity or aggressiveness of the game

This is an interesting point, and well worth digressing from our main theme for a moment to think about. Once you become familiar with the concept of standard deviation, and see it as a useful tool for qualifying and describing your hourly winning average, you will begin to see that poker strategy frequently involves walking a fine line between playing aggressively so as to maximize your win rate, and not taking unnecessary risks in order to minimize the variance or swings you experience.

When you begin thinking in terms of standard deviation, you will see that the answer to so many "How should I play this hand?" questions really depend on your own risk tolerance. As a player, you can choose between adopting a playing style designed to yield a higher win rate — and along with it, a much higher standard deviation — or winning just as much money by playing cautiously, although you'll have to put in more hours at the table. If this seems like an anomaly, it's not. It's also the reason why very aggressive, top notch players — those who take advantage of every edge, no matter how slight, in order to maximize their win rate — run a greater risk of going broke than work-a-day, grind-it-out professionals.

Statistical theory tell us that your results will be within plus or minus two standard deviations more than ninety-five percent of the time. Standard deviation increases by the square root of the number of hours played. If this statement is confusing to you, just take the square root of the number of hours you played. In this case, the square root of 900 (the number that when multiplied by itself, that yields 900) is 30. If you multiply 30 by your hourly standard deviation of 20 small bets, you get an overall standard deviation of 600. If you want boundaries with 95 percent certainty, you'll have to multiply this by two, to yield a result for two standard deviations. That number is 1,200.

If you divide 1,200 by the 900 hours you played, you'll see that your overall standard deviation equates to 1.3 small bets per hour, or $27 per hour. Suppose you've been beating that $20 - $40 game for $50 per hour, and after 900 hours you've won $45,000. Knowing this, what can you predict about the future?

If you multiply that $27 per hour overall standard deviation by 900 hours, you can add (and subtract) the result from your actual winnings of $45,000. If you do this, you'll come up with $69,300 on the high side and $20,700 on the low end. Here's what the standard deviation is telling you. If you won at the rate of $50 per hour for 900 hours and had a standard deviation of 20 small bets per hour, you can — with 95 percent certainty — expect to win between $20,700 and $69,300 (or between $23 and $77 per hour) in the future.

Sounds a little imprecise, doesn't it? That just goes to show you how very large the effect of short-term luck is in poker, even after 900 hours of play. If you want more precision from this statistical process, you need to keep records for more hours. Suppose you had the same results but played 2,000 hours instead of 900. Rather than an overall standard deviation of 1.3 small bets per hour, or $27 per hour, it would have been 0.6 small bets per hour, or $12 per hour. If, as before, you averaged winning at the rate of $50 per hour, you could expect to continue to win between $62 and $38 per hour. That's a lot more certainty. There's a pretty clear message here. It takes a rather long time to get into that elusive long run. Yet when you think about this, it does make perfect sense. The longer you play, the more likely it is that your results are sound predictive measures. After all, anyone can get lucky for a little while. In poker, however, that little while is often longer — much longer, in fact — than most of us think.

No credentials are required to be a professional poker player. No licensing or certification is needed. Anyone can do it. You can jump in if you dare, and who knows, you might succeed beyond your wildest dreams. But if you'd rather take a calculated risk before you give it a go, my advice is to be scrupulous about your record keeping, track your standard deviation and use it to provide some perspective on your win rate, and give yourself a fair tryout in the location you eventually plan to play before scorching the earth behind you.

Chapter 26

The Thinnest of Lines

Some gaps are wider than others. It's a long way across the Grand Canyon. Mark McGwire can hit a baseball twice as far as I can and then some. If the legend is true, and George Washington really did throw a silver dollar across the Potomac, he certainly didn't accomplish that feat at Mount Vernon, where he lived. The river is simply too wide at that point.

You'll never come close to hitting a golf ball like Tiger Woods, and if Michael Jordan spotted me 19 baskets in a 20 basket game of one-on-one, he'd still be a prohibitive favorite to beat me. It wouldn't even be close.

You get the idea. Some gaps are enormous chasms. Others are narrower. I've read that the average American lives two paychecks away from destitution. Even with a steady job, Mr. Average American is tiptoeing awfully close to the poverty line — and as anyone who's been downsized and outplaced can tell you, times tighten up rather quickly once a paycheck stops arriving.

Although many players are quick to employ the poker-is-a-sport metaphor, in reality it's a lot more like real life, particularly when one considers the gap between players of differing abilities. If you are a beginning or even an experienced player who has a hard time winning consistently, you can take solace in the fact that the gap between winning and losing poker players is not as wide as you may led yourself to believe. If you, on the other hand, are a winning player, be careful: You're probably not that much better than your adversaries.

Here's the good news. The gap between players is narrow, and narrow gaps can be crossed. That's the good news. The bad news is that even good players who develop leaks in either their game or their discipline frequently cross that gap in the wrong direction.

Statisticians will tell you that poker is a game where the variance, as measured by the standard deviation, is large when compared to the average amount of money won or lost per hour. This is math wonk jargon for saying that there's a lot of short-term luck in poker, and very good as well as very bad players will occasionally experience results that are completely at odds with their respective skill levels.

This sort of thing doesn't occur when gaps are wider. Gary Kasparov, I'm sure, could awaken from a five-day drunken stupor and annihilate almost anyone in a chess match without so much as a sobering cup of coffee. Some gaps are just too wide to cross.

A poker gap, however, is really quite slim. A good professional cash-game player is generally happy to win one big bet per hour. But the amount of money wagered to capture that one big bet can be substantial. In a $20-$40 game, for example, I fork over approximately $100 per hour in blinds, along with $14 in time collection. Each hand played to the river will cost $120, assuming the pot is not raised.

It's very likely that I will wager upwards of $600 every hour in my efforts to eke out a one-bet win — on average — from all this activity. When the line is so fine...so thin...so narrow, errors can be catastrophic. If I make a mistake that costs me the entire pot, I'll have to play one entire day to rectify that momentary lapse in judgment.

If I'm smart enough to save just one losing bet every hour, I can increase my hourly win rate from one to two big bets. After all, money saved is just as valuable as money won.

Good players don't have to go on tilt very long, nor is a catastrophic core meltdown required — just a slight list to the port or starboard will do — for them to cross that narrow line between winning and losing one big bet per hour.

In my opinion, game selection is the most important decision one makes at the poker table. I'm not the only one to hold this view either; others have said mush the same thing. Do you see why? In a soft game with loose, passive players, who are likely to call when they should fold, those extra bets gained can increase one's expected win rate from one to two, or even three big bets per hour.

While game selection is the most important decision one generally makes as a poker player, it goes without saying that discipline is essential to winning, even in loose, passive games. Without discipline it is easy — as well as all too common — for players to throw off money that needn't be lost. Think about it. Haven't you made calls you knew to be incorrect? Haven't you played hunches on occasion? You have, I have, and everyone I know has. I often wonder whether there is one single, solitary soul in the entire world who plays perfect poker all the time.

Even if there isn't, there's no reason why we shouldn't aspire to that ideal. Without a vision to guide us, how will we ever be able to improve? How can we assess the quality of our own play, unless it is measured against a standard of excellence we believe we can reach if we try.

The dark side of this equation is that poker players often succumb to negative forces. It happens all the time. Many players probably spend their entire poker career wandering aimlessly between winning and losing play. Even winning players spend some of their time playing like losers, and losing players do play well on occasion.

We've all seen this. A good run of cards can make an otherwise mediocre player start playing well. While a few bat beats — sometimes all it takes is one — can tilt a good player sufficiently far enough off center that he begins to chase, or play like a maniac, in an attempt to recoup lost money he believes should rightfully have been his.

The gap between mediocrity and good play cannot be explained completely away by relative differences in knowledge. After all, even novices know they shouldn't play a hand like 9-4. But sometimes they do. "It was suited," they'll say, "…and besides, I just had a feeling." But the cost of these momentary lapses can easily exceed one big bet per hour. When that happens, the gap begins to widen, and that narrowest of lines now looks like the Grand Canyon.

If poor plays are costing you too much money, there is just not enough skill differential between you and your opponents to overcome it. Winning play takes knowledge, to be sure. But it is predicated on a foundation of discipline, and a desire to win that is so strong, so compelling, that one cannot allow even a momentary lapse in judgment to distract their aim and focus.

When Ireland's Noel Furlong won the 1999 World Series of Poker, with countryman Padraig Parkinson taking third, I recalled a proverb in the Irish language that I read once. It's an adage that should be close to the hearts of poker players everywhere: Ni bhionn an rath ach mar a mbionn an smacht. (There is no luck except where there is discipline.)

Chapter 27

For the Record

Keeping Records

If you don't keep records, how will you know whether you're successful or not? The truth is, without accurate records, you'll never know how good a player you are. While most poker players don't keep accurate records, they'll also tell you they're winning players. They should know better. Since the majority of poker players are lifelong losers, there's a lot of self-deception taking place.

If you are serious about poker, you have to treat your game like a business or a profession. Every business keeps records. Without them, a business owner has no idea of what it costs to make, sell, or inventory a product, and no way of knowing whether his bottom line will be written in black or red.

Perhaps it's easier for the vast majority of poker players to avoid looking truth in the face. But if *you* intend to win money playing poker, you must keep abreast of the results you're achieving.

Fortunately, the kind of records you'll need to keep as a poker player are a lot simpler than the records maintained by business owners. In fact, they are much simpler than the kind of records you have to keep in order to prepare a simplified income tax return.

What Kind of Records Should I Keep?

In hold'em, as in every form of poker, you need to be concerned with two basic statistical parameters — your *win rate*, which is expressed as the average amount of money won or lost per hour, and the *standard deviation*, which measures the short-term fluctuations you face on the road to establishing an average hourly expectation.

Next time you play poker take a small pad with you. Record the amount of your buy-in. Then record the following information each hour:

1. Amount won or lost during that hour.

2. The game you're playing in (e.g., $2–$4 hold'em).

3. Total number of hours played that session.

When you arrive back home, you'll also want to record this cumulative information:

4. The amount won or lost for the entire year.

5. The total number of hours played during the year.

Now for the calculations. Computing your win or loss rate is simple. Just divide the amount of money won or lost by the number of hours played. This calculation will show you the average amount won or lost per hour played. In statistics, that figure is called the *mean*. If you play in different games, you might want to keep records on a game-by-game basis (to determine whether you're doing better at hold'em, or lowball, or Omaha) as well as on an overall basis.

Knowing how much you are winning or losing on an hourly basis is important. But it is equally important to know whether the mean is an accurate indicator of the data it represents.

Here's a case in point. Let's say San Francisco and Kansas City each have an average annual temperature of 65 degrees. San Francisco's, the temperature rarely becomes very warm or very cold, while Kansas City is very hot in the summer and extremely cold in winter. Although the mean annual temperature might be the same for both cities, there is greater variability in Kansas City than in San Francisco. Consequently, the mean temperature of 65 degrees is more representative of San Francisco's temperate climate than Kansas City's highly variable weather.

In poker, two players might each win an average of $15 per hour. One of these players might experience big wins and big losses very infrequently, while the other might experience substantial fluctuations to arrive at the same average winnings. The player who can achieve that win rate while putting less of his money at risk is generally better off.

To arrive at this measure of variability, we need to know more about *observed values* (the amount you won or lost each hour and recorded in your notebook) that were used to calculate your average wins or losses. Once we do, we can state with some certainty just how well the mean represents them. That's where the *standard deviation* comes in.

How Does the Standard Deviation Work?

If you haven't taken statistics, this term might seem awfully frightening. But it's not. Try thinking of the standard deviation as though it were an adjective modifying a noun (your hourly win rate). Here's an example: "She's wearing a dress." Dress, of course, is the noun. Now modify that sentence by adding any one of the following adjectives: "She's wearing a (sexy, blue, businesslike, grandmotherly, clinging, revealing, scandalous, see-through, designer, hideous, glamorous) dress. You can see how substituting one adjective for another can radically change the nature of the sentence. It's much the same with the relationship between the standard deviation and the mean.

If there were no dispersion at all in a distribution, all the observed values would be the same. No observed value would deviate from the mean. If, for example, it were exactly 72 degrees Fahrenheit for six days in a row, the mean temperature would be 72 degrees for that period, and there would be no variance between high and low. But, with dispersion, observed values do deviate from the mean, some by a little, some by a lot. The standard deviation is a way of indicating an "average" amount by which all the values deviate from the mean.

Which of these sets of values would you expect to have the larger standard deviation?

	"A"	"B"
	6	111
	24	114
	37	117
	49	118
	64	120
Mean	36	116

How to Calculate the Standard Deviation

The values in the left hand column are more dispersed (they deviate more from the mean) than those in the right hand column, so we can expect the standard deviation to be larger. Let's see how this works out.

Value	Deviation	Value	Deviation
6	-30	111	-5
24	-12	114	-2
37	+ 1	117	+1
49	+13	118	+2
64	+28	120	+4

We can't simply take an average (arithmetic mean) of the deviations because they will always add up to zero — since the negative deviations will cancel out the positive. To overcome this difficulty, we square each deviation (multiply the number by itself — thus 5 squared is equal to 5 times 5, or 25). This gets rid of the minus sign, since a "minus" multiplied by a "minus" is a "plus." So for the right hand column, we have:

Deviation from Mean	Deviation Squared
-5	25
-2	4
+1	1
+2	4
+4	16

The mean of these squared deviations is called the *Variance*:

$$\text{Variance} = \frac{25 + 4 + 1 + 4 + 16}{5} = \frac{50}{5} = 10$$

The variance is a measure with uses of its own. But it does have one disadvantage for everyday use: If the original values were in dollars (as they would be when you're calculating your hourly winnings or losses in a poker game), then the variance would be in dollars squared. This is hardly an easy concept to play around with. So, to get the *measure of dispersion* back into the same units as the *observed values*, we take the *square root* of the variance — and this is what we call the standard deviation.

Standard Deviation of the Distribution shown above = 3.16

The same calculations for the left-hand distribution yields a variance of 399.6, and a standard deviation of 19.99. Now that you've walked through the process of calculating a standard deviation, you can simplify the calculations.

Purchase a pocket calculator containing statistical functions. They can be bought for under $20 and will eliminate the time-consuming arithmetical steps. Better yet, if you have a personal computer, use any of the popular spreadsheet programs to store your data. Set up properly, all you'll have to enter are your hourly winnings or losses. But perhaps the best choice of all is a program such as Con-JelCo's *StatKing* for Windows which can be purchased inexpensively and is geared explicitly for recording your poker statistics. Then you can use the spreadsheet's or program's statistical capabilities to calculate your average hourly results (mean) and standard deviation on a cumulative basis.

Using the Standard Deviation to Analyze Poker Results

When you begin to analyze your poker results, you'll see that you're really trying to maximize your hourly winnings while minimizing your standard deviation. Simply stated, you'd like to win as much as you possibly can, while subjecting your bankroll to the smallest possible fluctuations.

This, of course, is a real conundrum. If you choose to take the risks required to maximize winnings, such as getting all those extra bets in whenever you believe you have the best of it, you tend to increase bankroll fluctuations, because you're not going to come out on top in every one of those marginal situations. In fact, because they're all very close calls, you'll probably wind up losing a lot of those confrontations. Let's face it, if you flopped a full house or some other equally monstrous hand, it's never a close call. You're going to get all the money in the pot you possibly can, because you're going to win the vast majority of such hands.

But when you're playing on the edge, you'll lose nearly as many hands as you win. You're hoping, of course, to win more often than not to maximize your winnings. But you're bound to experience fluctuations as you navigate poker's precarious waterways.

If calculating your standard deviation still seems burdensome, here's a shortcut. Calculate it for 100 hours of play. Then do the same thing a few months later. See if you've been able to reduce your standard deviation while increasing, or at least maintaining, your win rate. If you're able to do this, you've reduced the amount of money you put at risk. The gamble, in essence, has gotten better.

Life on the Edge: What's My Risk Tolerance?

From a statistical viewpoint, when you live on the edge you are flying in the face of minimizing your standard deviation. Because of this, you must come to terms with your own risk tolerance and how much of your bankroll you're willing to risk in order to gain marginal boosts in earnings. If you're not comfortable at a certain risk level, or playing on a short bankroll, you'd be better off minimizing your standard deviation rather than maximizing your winnings.

By avoiding marginal confrontations on the green-felt battlefield that require you to put additional money into the pot when it's a close decision or call, you can play on a shorter bankroll. If you're a winning player, you'll eventually win just as much money. It will just take more hours of play to reach your goals.

There is no right or wrong answer. Some people are comfortable with a high level of risk and have the bankroll to accommodate the fluctuations that inevitably accompany their play. Others are not. In fact, you'll frequently hear players bemoaning the fact that they are at a table with all live ones. "I wish there were two or three good, tight players at the table," they're wont to say, "because they bring more stability to the game and my good hands tend to hold up."

From a statistical perspective, this comment is a cry for a smaller standard deviation, and a willingness to accept a slightly smaller win rate. Even without a knowledge of statistics, these players have learned that when they operate on the edge, or when they're in a jam-up game with a lot of maniacs, the price they pay for an increased win rate is usually a significantly larger increase in the fluctuations they can expect.

As the win rate increases marginally, the standard deviation tends to fluctuate dramatically. That's the reason Mason Malmuth says that expert players stand a better chance of going broke than good ones. (The bad player, of course, will inevitably go broke no matter what he does, since he doesn't have the skills required to beat the game.)

How Should You Balance Your Win Rate Against the Standard Deviation?

What does this question mean to you as a player? Do you live on the edge, or do you seek whatever safety net might be available? As long as you can afford to play the game you're in, this becomes a matter of personal choice. Only you can decide how much uncertainty you're comfortable with. If you elect to push every advantage, no matter how small, expect significantly higher fluctuations than you'd experience if you were willing to trade off some of that win rate for a bit more stability. If you elect to maximize your win rate, then you'll need a larger bankroll to play the game.

Keeping Up With Record Keeping

One of the tough things about keeping records is simply keeping them up to date. After a tough loss, it can be very difficult to record it in your record book, where it stares you in the face each time you glance at it. But if you don't keep records, you'll only delude yourself about the results you've achieved at the table. If you are playing just for enjoyment, and don't really care whether you win or lose, then by all means excuse yourself from the drudgery. But if you are a winning player, or aspire to be one, you must record and analyze your results.

If these concepts are new to you, or if they have struck a responsive chord, you'll want to read Mason Malmuth's *Gambling Theory and Other Topics*. Malmuth provides a thorough discussion of the relationship between a player's win rate and standard deviation, as well as the ramifications it has on your bankroll requirements.

Chapter 28

How Lessons From Poker Apply to Everyday Life

*I*s there a writer who ever played the game who hasn't observed that poker is a metaphor for life?

A *metaphor for life*. If true, there can be major life lessons everyone can take away from the poker table — lessons which once learned and applied to the real world make it manifestly easier for a poker player to survive in a world populated by those who haven't learned these advanced strategies for living.

Be Selective, But Be Aggressive

How true. In the real world you have to pick your battles, carefully choose when to retreat (fold'em) and when to draw your proverbial line in the sand (hold'em). History is replete with examples. General Robert E. Lee, in the face of overwhelming supremacy in men, munitions, and technology, was able to keep the Confederacy's cause alive for as long as he did because he picked his battles carefully. He did not engage the Union Army at every opportunity. Instead, he selected opportunities where he believed he could negate the inherent Union advantages and overcome them.

In fact, during the early stages of the war, Union General George McClellan was unwilling to commit his troops, even when the odds were strongly in his favor. Like a player who is overly cautious (tight), he was constantly run off the best hand by General Lee. McClellan ultimately suffered the military equivalent of losing all his chips — he was sacked by President Lincoln who, knowing his man held most of the big cards, wondered why he wouldn't play a hand and therefore couldn't win.

Always Observe Your Opponents

If you can pick up tells in a poker game — where players take pains not to broadcast them — think how easy it should be to read people *away* from the table. Yet how many of us really do this? Your boss is in a nasty, irritable mood. Wouldn't you be better off feigning an emergency and postponing your annual performance review until he's in better humor? You always stand a better chance of winning when you hold a strong hand. Tackle a tough project, close that sale, or make some customer so happy that he calls your boss and tells him how valuable you are. Once you've done that you're holding strong cards — strong enough to stand up to your annual review.

Try it in your social life. You don't have to be an expert on body language to realize that you're not getting to first base with a woman who's got her legs crossed, arms folded, and is leaning away from you with an indifferent expression on her face. It's time to try a new strategy, or be selective, fold your hand, and wait for some new cards to be dealt.

Do the Pot Odds Offset the Odds Against Making Your Hand?

No winning player would draw to a hand with 5-to-1 odds against making it, when the pot only promises a 3-to-1 payoff. Instead, the winning player waits until the pot promises a payoff better than 5-to-1 before investing his money. The same holds is true away from the table. While real life payoffs can vary, usually your investment is time. Is it worth your time to spend half a day trying to make a small sale, without the promise of greater rewards down the road, or are you better off courting one of your bigger, better customers?

Whenever you analyze similar circumstances, the answers are obvious. Still, people fritter away large amounts of time, often not realizing that they are being horribly unproductive. Office workers sometimes spend hours dealing with problems and issues which may be urgent to them, but are neither significant nor important to company goals.

Better time management frees you from dealing with small-payoff issues over which you have little control. If you aspire to success, look for key spots that allow you to capitalize on an opportunity, rather than ones that force you to fight small, insignificant brush fires.

Once you're able to step back from the daily demands of urgent-though-unimportant issues, you'll be able to see opportunities as easily as you saw that spending time with important customers was more productive than spinning your wheels on tasks with insignificant payoffs.

Have a Plan

If you have no set standards, and adopt an any-two-cards-can-win philosophy, you'll soon go broke. You need to know in advance which cards you're going to play, what position you'll play various combinations of starting cards from, and how you'll handle different opponents. We provided a Start Chart earlier in this book for just that purpose. But in the real world, if you don't plan, you're simply a leaf in the wind. Traveling in a random direction will get you somewhere, though probably not where you hoped to go.

Poker teaches you to have a plan, to have an agenda, and to pursue it aggressively. In the real world, if you don't have your own agenda, you'll soon become part of someone else's. In fact, I'd guess that if you examined every person who joined a cult, you'd find very few of them had a plan, an agenda, or a set of governing values to guide them.

Do You Have an Out?

When I was 12 years old my arch enemy was an overgrown 13-year-old named Zimp. He was always threatening to beat the crap out of me, and I had no doubt he could do it. But I had an out. Zimp was big; Zimp was strong. Zimp also was slow. Since I could out-run him, outride him on my bicycle, out-climb him on any trees, or garage roofs he'd try to chase me over, I had an out. As long as I never allowed myself to become cornered in a blind alley, I knew I could make it to adulthood with all my vital parts intact.

I had another enemy, a kid named Skinny Vinny. Now I could take Vinny seven days a week, but he could outrun me. I seldom caught him. Had Vinny and Zimp been card players they would have known that even though I was a favorite against each of them individually (I could take Vinny, and I could outrun Zimp), if the two of them ever teamed up, I was dead meat. All it would have taken was for Vinny to run me down and keep me engaged until Zimp arrived to toss me a beating. Lucky for me that neither one had an ounce of brains, and never got together to conspire on how to take out their mutual enemy.

Next time you're holding a pair of kings or aces, and thinking about just calling instead of raising to limit the field, remember Zimp and Vinny. They never got the better of me because each chose to face me heads up — and I had the outs. If they took me on together, I'd have gone from a favorite individually, to an underdog against their collective efforts.

Most of my childhood was spent in Brooklyn, where street smarts were required learning at an early age. Maybe these street smarts helped me to learn poker by providing the discipline required to play it well. But poker also gave me more street smarts than I would have garnered had I never played it. Who knows, maybe poker and real life are mutually self-enhancing. If you keep playing the game, and listen to the messages coming your way across the card table, you'll not only win at poker, you'll win at life. Bet on it!

Chapter 29

Where Do You Go From Here

Having read this far, you might think you've learned enough to knock'em dead at the tables. Were this but true, I would be a wealthier man — and so, quite shortly, would you!

This book is basic training. There's much more to learn, much more to read — and you'll need hours and hours at the poker table to convert your book learning into real know-how. In *Poker Essays*, Mason Malmuth lists seven books he considers "...absolutely must-reading for anyone striving for success in this game."

There have, in fact, been so many good poker books written in the past decade (as well as a few really dreadful ones) that I wondered if there was enough literature to build a poker curriculum ... just as if we were going to construct a college course — or series of courses — on poker. To construct a poker curriculum it is important to identify the worthwhile books as well as their order of study.

I really believe novices can learn to play well and learn to do it rather quickly. To do so they need a desire to learn, coupled with sufficient hours at the table to apply their knowledge under various game conditions. They also have to maintain their discipline. If you're a new player, here is your reading list. If you're an old hand, consider this a refresher course.

Basic Reading For All Players

Poker for Dummies by Richard D. Harroch and Lou Krieger, is — at the risk of sounding immodest — a sound introduction to all forms of poker played in cardrooms and casinos. It's easy to read, easy to follow, and a terrific book for newbies and experienced players alike.

The Theory of Poker (formerly titled *Winning Poker*) by David Sklansky. To learn anything well, you need a solid grounding in theory. This book provides it. Moreover, it is not oriented to just one game. Poker theory and strategic concepts are discussed and exemplified against a variety of games and situations. No matter what game you might decide to specialize in, this book is going to be helpful.

Super/System — A Course in Power Poker by Doyle Brunson. This is the Bible of "how-to" books and it covers the majority of poker games. First published in 1978, it is currently being revised to include new game variations and structures. Super/System, the first edition, is still the second book in your syllabus.

For Stud Players

If you're a beginning seven-card stud player, your next book is *7-Card Stud — The Complete Course in Winning at Medium and Lower Limits* by Roy West.

To really learn the game, you should follow West's book with *Championship Stud* by Dr. Max Stern, Linda Johnson, and Tom McEvoy, as well as *Seven-Card Stud For Advanced Players* by David Sklansky, Mason Malmuth, and Ray Zee. Both of these are the state-of-the-art as far as stud books go, and it will give the reader a big edge over most players encountered in small- and mid-limit games.

For Hold'em Players

If you want to learn more about hold'em after reading this book, read my second book, *More Hold'em Excellence: A Winner for Life*, as well as *Winning Low-Limit Hold'em*, by Lee Jones. These three books will provide a solid foundation for becoming a winning hold'em player in any game. You should also read *Hold'em Poker* by David Sklansky, followed by *Hold'em Poker for Advanced Players* by David Sklansky and Mason Malmuth. These two books will take you from the basics through some very advanced strategic concepts.

Caro's 12 Days to Hold'em Success. Designed to reinforce positive playing habits. Playable hands and advice on when to call, raise, pass, or fold in a variety of situations.

Caro's Professional Hold'em Report. Suggests ways to improve your game; what to stay with before and after the flop; position; pot-limit and no-limit games; and when to call, raise, or check.

For All Players

If you read the books in the order shown above, and supplement that with live play, then reread and think about the contents in terms of what you encounter at the table, you stand a chance of becoming a winner. The books that follow will also help you significantly; not necessarily in technique, but in understanding the context in which the game is played.

Caro's Fundamental Secrets of Poker by Mike Caro covers all the tips dispensed at his extremely popular poker seminars — and a few more. If you want to know how to choose a seat at the poker table ... whether sad sounds are terrifying ... and why, if they're helpless and can't defend themselves, you're in the right game, this book is a must read.

Gambling Theory and Other Topics by Mason Malmuth is one I consider must-reading. If you don't learn the concept of non-self-weighting strategies, the implications of the standard deviation on your win rate, and the bankroll required to play in different limit games, you are likely to spend a lifetime personalizing losing streaks and bad beats — wondering why they happen only to you.

After you read this book, you will clearly see that these events are (from a statistical point of view) to be expected. This book gave me a much broader perspective to assess my own game, while putting my two years of college statistics in a usable format.

Getting The Best of It by David Sklansky deals with overall gambling concepts, and it contains a section devoted to poker. Even if you're not mathematically-inclined, this book has an excellent section on the mathematics of gambling. It is easily understood even by those who claim to be numerically illiterate.

Caro's Book of Tells along with the video *Caro's Pro Poker Tells* both by Mike Caro contain the best available information on body language at the table.

With all of poker's behavioral aspects, it's not surprising that quite a few psychologists have chosen to write about the game. *The New Gambler's Bible* by Arthur S. Reber, Ph.D.; *The Psychology of Poker* by Alan N. Schoonmaker, Ph.D., and *Inside the Poker Mind* by John Feeney, Ph.D., are all must reads for players who are serious about their game.

Though not a book, *Sklansky ... the Video* is 90 minutes of general poker concepts and strategies from a master strategist and theoretician, along with specific advice for hold'em, seven-card stud, and Omaha high-low split. It will benefit beginners and experienced players. New truths seem to unfold from this video each time I watch it.

Another useful video is *Caro's Power Poker Seminar* Video. It presents strategy, psychology, and statistics in a colorful — sometimes humorous — language that's aimed at both beginners and experienced players.

If you want to supplement the technical material with some books which will give you the flavor of poker, then I recommend *The Biggest Game In Town* by A. Alvarez, which is about the World Series of Poker and its participants.

You'll also enjoy *Big Deal, A Year As a Professional Poker Player* by Anthony Holden. In this book, Anthony "London Tony" Holden, the esteemed biographer of Prince Charles, as well as literary and poker-playing companion of A. Alvarez (in what must be the best home game in England) takes a year off to play poker tournaments and ring games in Las Vegas, London, the Isle of Man, and other exotic locales. Holden's perception, wit, and self-deprecating sense of humor make it a real page-turner.

Four works by the late David Spanier, *Total Poker*, *Welcome to the Pleasuredome: Inside Las Vegas*, *The Little Book of Poker*, and *Inside the Gambler's Mind* each deal with the gambling and poker environment — though each book approaches it from a different perspective. All three are well worth reading.

Bobby Baldwin's *Winning Poker Secrets* will not make you a better hold'em player, but it does give you a flavor of one player's struggle to make it to the top as a professional.

These books are enough to give you an undergraduate degree in poker. Like any recent college graduate, you'll find the "real world" to be different, and education at an entirely new level will begin at the table. If you're new to poker, these books will give you the basics you need. They are books that you should continue to reread. Many of the concepts and strategies are very sophisticated, and you will not grasp all of their potential implications in one reading. In fact, the more you learn, the more applicable many of these books become. You'll find yourself reading and digesting them in an iterative process of "read, play, think."

If you have a computer, you can speed your way up the learning curve by working with some of the poker programs that are available. I recommend *Turbo Texas Hold'em* as today's state-of-the-art poker software. Additionally, you should read *Card Player* and *Poker Digest*. Both are published biweekly, and together they should be your up-to-the-minute guide to the world of poker.

Never stop. Winning at poker demands continuous learning. The process of learning and thinking about poker ought never cease. And you know what? The more you learn, the more you'll win, and the more enjoyment the game provides. So study up. Then go out and play some hold'em and knock'em dead. Have a wonderful time ... *And keep flopping aces.*

Lou Krieger learned poker at the tender age of seven, while standing at his father's side during the weekly Thursday night game held at the Krieger kitchen table in the blue-collar Brooklyn neighborhood where they resided. Always adept at sports and games, Lou's natural abilities enabled him to keep his head above water during the high school and college poker games he frequently played in.

But it wasn't until his first visit to Las Vegas that Lou took poker seriously. "I didn't like Las Vegas at first. Blackjack was boring, and I knew the odds were against the players shooting dice or playing any of the other table games. Then I discovered a poker table tucked into a small corner of the Desert Inn where we were staying. I bought into a low-limit seven-card stud game and managed — with a good deal of luck — to break even. While playing stud, I noticed out of the corner of my eye another game that looked to be a lot more fun. *It was Texas hold'em.*

"I left the stud game, watched the hold'em game for about thirty minutes, and sat down to play. One hour and $100 later, I was hooked. I didn't mind losing. It was the first time I played the game. I *expected* to lose. But I didn't like feeling like a dummy, so I bought every book on poker I could find.

"I studied. I played. I studied and played some more. Before long I was playing and winning regularly, and I haven't had a losing year since I began keeping records."

In the early '90s Lou Krieger began writing a column called *On Strategy* for *Card Player.* Aimed squarely at hold'em players, the column is chock full of advice for beginners, low-limit, and even experienced mid-limit hold'em players.

When not writing about poker, Lou — who resides in Long Beach — can be found playing Texas hold'em in the card casinos of Southern California.

ConJelCo is a publisher based in Pittsburgh, Pennsylvania that specializes in books and software for the serious gambler. In addition to this book, ConJelCo publishes the companion book *More Hold'em Excellence* also by Lou Krieger as well as *Winning Low-Limit Hold'em* by Lee Jones, *Las Vegas Blackjack Diary* by Stuart Perry, *Video Poker–Optimum Play* by Dan Paymar, *Serioius Poker* by Dan Kimberg, and several software products including *Blackjack Trainer* for the Macintosh and Windows, *Ken Elliott's CrapSim* for DOS, and *StatKing* for Windows, software for keeping poker statistics.

ConJelCo periodically publishes a newsletter, *The Intelligent Gambler*, sent free to our customers. *The Intelligent Gambler* carries articles by our authors as well as other respected authors in the gambling community. In addition, it is the source of information about new ConJelCo products and special offers.

ConJelCo also sells books, software and videos from other publishers. If you'd like a free catalog or to be put on the mailing list for *The Intelligent Gambler* you can write to us at:

> ConJelCo
> 132 Radcliff Dr.
> Pittsburgh, PA 15237

Our phone number is 800-492-9210 (412-492-9210 outside of the U.S.), and our fax number is 412-492-9031.

ConJelCo is on the Internet. You can send electronic mail to us at *orders@conjelco.com*. From the World Wide Web you can reach us at URL *http://www.conjelco.com*. On our web server you'll find a complete, annotated, ConJelCo catalog, demos of software by ConJelCo and others, and lots of other goodies for the serious gambler.

The Lou Krieger Start Chart

With only 169 different two-card starting combinations, learning to play them is not as tough as you might think. Each of the 169 two-card holdings is shown on this chart. Pairs of the same rank have equal value before the flop. So do similarly-suited cards. For example, prior to the flop, 9♠9♦ is equal to 9♥9♣, and K♣Q♣ is just as worthy as K♦Q♦. But if the flop contains three diamonds, then the K♦Q♦ might be priceless, and the K♣Q♣ unplayable.

Hands are arrayed in descending order. Playable hands in early position begin with big pairs and big connectors, which fan out from the chart's upper left-hand corner. Middle- and late-position hands are tucked under the curve formed by the early-position hands, and unplayable two-card holdings are located toward the right hand side of the charts. With a little work you should be able to commit this to memory.

If you're new to the game, have been playing indiscriminately, or have an any-two-cards-can-win philosophy, you may believe these starting requirements are too tight. To the contrary, they are somewhat loose. The strategic concepts embodied in this chart are not immutable marching orders. If the pot has been raised in front of you, tighten up significantly on the hands you play, particularly from early position.

Don't fall into the trap of predictable play. Consider a hand like T♥9♥. Just because it may be a playable early position hand in a normal game doesn't mean you must play it. In a game with frequent raises or shorthanded pots, it is unplayable. It is a very speculative hand—one best played inexpensively, from late position. Ideally, you'd want to play this kind of hand on the button, with seven or eight callers ahead of you, in a pot that hasn't been raised. Now it's worth a flyer. You can always toss your hand away whenever the flop is unfavorable.

Remember this: The key to success at hold'em is to **Be Selective... But Be Aggressive!**